Wisdoms

Also by Dorothy Maclean

The Living Silence

To Hear the Angels Sing

The Soul of Canada

To Honor the Earth

Choices of Love

Seeds of Inspiration:
Deva Flower Messages

Call of the Trees

Come Closer:
Messages from the God Within

Wisdoms
Earlier Editions

First edition undated
58 messages - Published by the Findhorn Foundation Copyright © Dorothy Maclean under the name Divina
First edition 1970
100 messages - Published by the Findhorn Foundation Copyright © Dorothy Maclean
Second edition April 1975
Third edition October 1977
Fourth edition 1979
Fifth edition 1991
Reprinted by Colombiere Center with permission from Dorothy Maclean

Wisdoms

Dorothy Maclean

Wisdoms

Edited by Freya Secrest
Design and Layout by Jeremy Berg
Cover Art and Interior Illustrations by Dorothy Maclean

Published by Lorian Press
2204 E Grand Ave.
Everett, WA 98201

ISBN 0-936878-09-6
978-0-936878-09-6

Maclean, Dorothy
Wisdoms / Dorothy Maclean

First Lorian Edition: March 2008

Printed in the United States of America

5 4 3 2 1 0 9 8 7 6

www.lorian.org

Note: *The interior illustrations in this book and the cover are all from the artistic hand of Dorothy Maclean. Most of these pieces were originally painted with watercolors as was the cover of this book.*

*This book is dedicated to Sheena
who helped me find inner Wisdoms*

$\mathcal{I}$n 1954, after earlier having the wonderful experience of knowing that God was within, I was asked from within to "Stop, listen and write." When I eventually did this, I received inspiring experiences which I put into words and wrote down. These became the pole star of my life, and gave me the help, training, joy and love which I needed for any situation. Basically I was asked to be more loving in my life. I followed this advice as much as I could for the ten years before coming to Findhorn. There I was also told I had a job to communicate with Nature and when I did, we received help from Nature beings, the angels or devas, in our attempts to grow vegetables in sand. Our cooperation with Nature in the Findhorn Garden grew from following their suggestions.

Still, I was needing and receiving help from within to put more love in my life, as the messages in this book show. In 1971 I was told to be more that just obedient to these inner prompting and to act more maturely on my own initiative. Whenever I needed help, though, I still received it.

The contents of this book, one hundred messages chosen from June 1970 to December 1971, have been slightly edited for republication. May you be inspired, as others have been, by these messages and from your own still small voice within.

Dorothy Maclean 2008

*F*eel into the varied chitter of the birds this morning, not into the sounds themselves but into the quality of nature behind them. It is clear, outgoing, immediate, happy and individually expressing the common sharing. You can hardly hear the sounds because you have shut the windows; they become stronger as you become quiet and focus on them. How easily are the sounds lost when you turn your attention to something else! But listen attentively and beautiful soaring notes are heard.

The same process is repeated when you listen to My voice within. At first you hear various voices and lean in various directions, perhaps wondering which is Mine. Then the window of doubt is pulled down and you hear nothing; you do not want to hear the false. As you focus more attentively in the silence, a clear voice comes and you soar, for it is My voice and I always lift. Of course when you come to Me in desperation, as most of you do at first, your concentrated desire or need cuts through all processes and veils and your answer is there-naturally, for I AM always here.

Naturally the birds and the bees and the rest of creation send forth My voice each in its own way. They do not have to seek to find Me; they have no thought barriers. But you, made in My image, can even turn those thought barriers to good by using thought as My servant, having divorced it from your own use. There are many in the world today who believe that thought is the enemy - and this is truth, a truth to be gone into deeply and still more deeply until all past thought has gone. But as everything has purpose, so has thought, which, when used creatively for Me, manifests worlds. Up to now thought has been the servant of separated humanity and has been used to create still more separation. Now in the new I can direct thought through you towards unity.

Before this can happen there must be no doubt in you as to My voice; you must be as clear about it as the rest of creation which knows not doubt nor choice. That is up to you. I am here, immense, all there is within and without. Nothing else is, accept that and let My voice be heard.

June 13, 1970

$\mathcal{T}$here is nowhere where I am not. You may tune into a flower, a caterpillar, the sky, and I will be there speaking indirectly. You open your eyes and see My handiwork; you listen and hear My creation. Through all the senses I am evident, if your consciousness is alive enough. But from within I speak directly in a voice from depths you cannot plumb, and from within I fill all space. In the silence My presence fills you, and you wonder why you cannot act from the same consciousness all the time. You can, and you do at times and those times are increasing. Cease denigrating yourself and let Me be in you. Cease dwelling on past patterns of weakness; I am here now, mighty. Cease blaming your circumstances or anyone else for what you are. Those circumstances you have drawn to yourself and in them it is perfect for you. I am in them, whether you consider them good or evil, and in them in particular you can find My mighty presence and become imbued with Me.

In this time of communion I am all there is to you. At other times this is equally true, but you have let your awareness become limited, and generally limited to something to do with yourself, to some comparison between yourself and others. How ridiculous, when within you is all there is! Whatever barrage of facts you may marshal, every one is overcome by the one fact that I am here now, whatever you do and wherever you are. My authority is within, and from within you can rearrange your world.

Now relax in My presence. Do not strain over it. It simply is, and is always available. Trust it and it will never fail you. Why continue to perpetuate your weaknesses when I am here? You are new, for I am here. Love Me, love My creation, love your situation, and we will be One always.

June 14 1970

$\mathscr{T}$he pattern for each one of you is very alive within, trying to express itself and waiting for you to cooperate with it. But you, unlike a flower, have your own individual likes and dislikes, with the world imposing its accepted ways until the pattern is unable to fulfill itself. In a flower a petal curls up or down or in, according to its intrinsic design, but in the human world current fashion dictates outer appearance and thinking, and individual choice makes the selection.

How do you know when individual choice is according to your own pattern? I can tell you that from within and confirm it in many ways, but first you must have no choice. The world and human nature are in such a state of separation from Me, from the basic pattern, that you without Me are incapable of choosing what is right for you in any field at all. Although you all have natural leanings one way or another, these have been so used for narrow-minded purposes instead of for the whole that they are no longer a true guide. Only I within you am a true guide, and I can only guide you when you choose to seek Me. Choose outwardly and you are open to every wind of chance, to any intelligent entity, to you know not what.

You say that you lose your individuality when you give up choice. No, you find it. Like a flower, you have a basic pattern which is perfect. Do you see humans without faults? Not now in the world of free choice. With Me, who am love and all-knowing, wholeness is, and I can tell you the perfect step to make in each moment. I radiate it out from deep within you. Your choices change all the time. I within am constant, perpetually giving you the suitable answer for you in all situations, and I do not do it coldly. You feel that you are at home at last. Everything is right, for you are beginning to find your real pattern. Together we make all worlds new.

June 16, 1970

$\mathcal{Y}$esterday I said that you, humanity, are incapable of choosing what is right for you, such is the state of separation from your basic pattern, until you choose Me. When you have given up other choices, then no effort is involved and there is no constant rushing to Me to find your answers. You simply find yourself giving forth those answers without thought. You find things working out in a way that would be miraculous compared with your previous state, and you find great peace and joy.

Giving up separated choice is the vital step of the time, and one that is greatly misunderstood. It is couched in negative language but it is most positive. It is becoming truly creative, for it is a tuning into the power which I am within you, the power which you are, this alive, radiating power which fits in perfectly with and is basically the same as every other part of creation. In your limited state of free choice, which is still the great gift that distinguishes you from other planetary life, your choice is liable to be the same as that of your neighbors, i.e, the biggest, the best or the most, in some way . But when you simply let your pattern work out in you, accepting all that comes to you as right, as it is bound to be—in other words, when you have no other desire—the power and creativity and life in you are free to go out unhindered and different in each. It simply is, and is a source of surprise to yourself, for you are full of riches! You have unplumbed depths to discover.

You know the principle that when you give up something for the greater good, it is returned a hundredfold. What could be more hundredfold than My will, which is then yours, which suits every occasion? Simplicity itself is then yours, while you fulfill the finest scientific laws, laws beyond the range of the mind. You cease to separate yourself and, in so doing, become a unique unit linked with all other units. I am one and I am many, and so are you when you let Me be in you. The choice is yours.

June 17, 1970

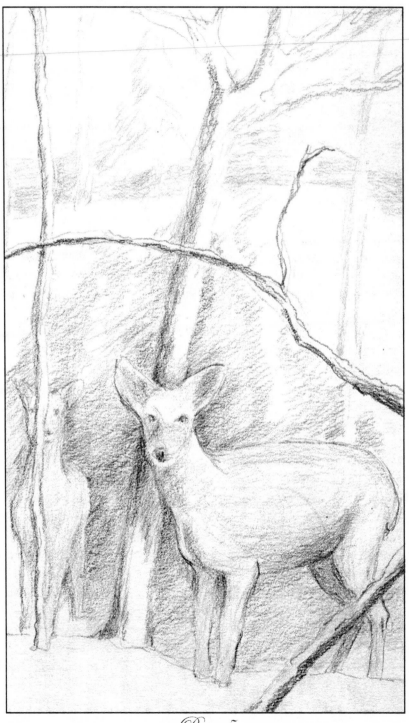

$\mathscr{E}$ach of you, to be fully yourself, would not only be content with your lot, your pattern, but would be overjoyed with it. If you are a small cog, you will enjoy being a small cog. If you see someone else with a greater awareness, you will still know that you, in your so-called limitation, can be used by Me exactly as I want to use you, and that perhaps your very limitation is right. A masterpiece of painting need not be large to be perfect of its kind, and each of you has the seeds of perfection.

Of course you are growing, learning and expanding. You learn by finishing as best you can that which is at hand, and then going on. You feel frustrated if you attempt something beyond your capabilities and never finish it correctly. You need the joy in the completion of work, whether it be a work of art, a message from Me, a meal, the typing of a letter. All of you fits in beautifully. All of you have jobs to do. When I am active within you, whatever you do brings satisfaction and rightness to your being.

Are you dissatisfied with your lot? Then you are somehow blocking that pattern within. No one but you can block it because you are a sacred unit, individualized and given freedom, and no one but you can unblock it. It may be a very small block; for instance it may be nothing but the fact that you compare your lot with that of another and think someone else's lot is better than yours. How ridiculous! You cannot judge what you see of anyone else's pattern, why they seem to be having an easy time or why the opposite seems to be happening to you. You can accept and make the most of what comes to you. You can make a wonderful pattern in the framework that is presented to you, and you can enjoy it. The master workman in any trade does just that, and you are all master workmen, for I am within each one of you.

Yes, I am within each one of you, in the limitation of the framework which you are. Then cannot a masterpiece be produced by you? Of course it can, when you choose to work towards it with the tools you have. You may be able to manifest better tools, but the framework is what you have already drawn to yourself. As it is dealt with in wholeness, so does it change. Accept what you are, and be happy, joyous and content in your work. So do you and your work grow, and I grow in you, and all is very, very well.

June 20, 1970

$\mathcal{L}$isten. The air is full of sound, and you know that it is also full of radio and television waves that can be turned into sound. Listen within and there is also fullness, anticipation and movement of sound. Through the one sense of hearing there is contact with many, many worlds, and it is the same with the other senses. You are like a telephone exchange, connected in all directions, but normally you make use of but few of your wires. Normally you are plugged into one set of them, to the ordinary physical level.

You are born because it is right for you to be plugged into this world and experience its communications. You are here to learn mastery here, and then move on to other realms. The past tendency has been to exclude some other levels, particularly the physical. Nothing should be excluded. You are neither to wander around dreaming of finer things, nor to ignore the finer vibrations. Balance is essential, exciting and a work of art itself, especially at this time. You have to be fully extended to be able to find that changing balance. Your mind cannot often help you, for you are dealing with new awarenesses. Your feelings or intuition can only help if you choose the whole and get out of the habit of believing that you are the main telephone exchange on earth! I within can always tell you, for I know all things.

When you have learned right discrimination, or mastery over certain things, with that knowing you can then you go on to something else, and then need Me again. There is no end of the learning, there is no end to your need of Me and your greater and greater blending with Me. I am the core, the pivot, of your life. I am that incredible activity around and within, and I am also the central point of peace within all that. All these worlds, for which I have given you the faculties to translate into sound or sight or feel, are My creation. Therefore I am the common factor in all of them, and am your point of rest and springboard for action.

You can get lost in any of these worlds, particularly the physical, without Me. You are inclined to divorce Me from your burdens instead of realizing that with Me those stumbling blocks become stepping stones. You are generally switched on to a certain idea about things and problems. When you switch to Me, a broader viewpoint is presented and a way is shown.

So realize that whatever your situation, on whatever level, I am the vital factor in the midst of it. Bring Me into all you do.

June 22, 1970

"*Truth* is all there is" or "The truth will set you free." You come across such statements, but what do they really mean, especially as truth is relative. What is truth to you one day is not necessarily true the next. The words, "I am Truth" are better, for then I am brought in with the dynamic of the present tense, the dynamic of the radiating life within you. "I am truth": you could go into the ramifications of the word "truth" but it fades into nothingness beside the "I" which you are.

What is truth? Jesus did not answer that question, and it would not have helped his situation if he had said "I am the truth" as he said elsewhere. I am truth: I am all things to all men. Truth is only theory, possible truth, until it is lived or put into practice. You are to live "I am truth" in every possible way, and you begin and end that with Me.

This is not impractical mysticism. Try it. You want to know the truth about some situation? I can give it to you. I can give the perfect answer for you - and then you must act on my words. If you do not act on them, that possible truth eludes you. "I Am" is the operative phrase, now, and if you miss your lesson of the moment, miss your possible truth, circumstances will again insist that you at some time incorporate that truth into your being. You can see other people's faults and where they fall down in incorporating truth into their beings, but that does not help them or you, although it may point the way. They must experience that truth. I am in that moment of truth; I Am Truth, I AM. Be not afraid of any truth about yourself; this is where truth sets you free. No matter what you have been, I am here within, closer now, one barrier removed, alive within and knowing all things.

Turn to Me for your truth. Make straight your paths to Me, for I AM TRUTH.

June 24, 1970

$\mathcal{T}$he whole planet is on the move. Unrest is everywhere, old patterns are crumbling, old standards have vanished. The young are roaming the world seeking. There is great experimentation in every form of art. Politics and economics no longer apply as before. The very food you eat is being questioned. In every department of life there is a seething as the new comes in. Humans look around frantically in all media for solutions, when all the time the newness and the solutions are within them. I am within them, coming out as never before and upsetting the many barriers they have put up between us on every level. I am life itself, in all things but particularly expressing in humanity—and you cannot stop life from radiating out.

There will continue to be chaos everywhere until you stop trying to reconcile outer activities and, instead, reconcile your inner life with Me. I am this enormous newness within, bursting out, refusing to accept the limitations you put on Me. Your thoughts limit you beyond measure, and you look around and limit others. But that is going, for I am breaking through. You, the separate you, no matter what I may do through you, can take no credit nor add any feathers to your cap, for I am the doer; it is My activity in all. You can let either more or less of Me be in you. You are free to choose.

My bursting life within is something for you to accept and let be. Do not go on in your old ways; expand into newness. Aid the new age. I am here, immanent; let old limitations go. Feel the joy, the activity, of the new, and let go the sterile old. Let the old forms break around you; they do not matter because you have Me. I am all you have ever had—but you did not know it. Know it and claim nothing but Me. I am the new and I am you, which is all you need. Replace all the old with Me and let the newness come marching in.

That is a fine martial note on which to stop this message, but do not stop. Continue with Me. Let me be in all your moments. Everything is on the move, every part of life. I am that life, be with Me.

June 25, 1970

*W*hy should I be so deeply hidden in each of you when I am so obvious in the rest of creation? You look at the perfection of flowers and see My handiwork. You see me in the wonders revealed by the microscope or the telescope, in the grace of a cat or the beauty of a sunset. But you shy away from the thought of Me in yourself or in another human. You acknowledge Me as a mighty Being somewhere, somehow, and within all things, but when it comes to that Supreme Being expressing itself in words through you, oh no, that is blasphemous!

This reaction results from the development of the mind, with which you become conscious of self and of everything else as separate from yourself. Humanity has been in the consciousness of the separated self for many ages and has built up its life on this premise. You have ruled your world by thought emanating from a sense of separation. Some members and great teachers have broken through these thought-forms back to the truth and simplicity of their oneness with Me, having experienced this in consciousness. Yet humanity as a whole holds firmly to the idea that you are the center and originator of your activity, rather as in the Middle Ages the earth was considered to be the center of the system and Galileo was persecuted for saying that the sun was the center. Few believed him at the time, for they could not conceive of such an upsetting idea. Gradually the truth was confirmed, and now you laugh at the absurdity of the belief of that time.

You know that I am within you because you have experienced it, and nothing can take away that knowing. With many arguments the separated mind can try to make nonsense of this fact, or it can try to prove the point. It can do neither, because I am beyond its terms of reference. But remember that the case against Me is a popular and powerful one at the moment, and be not surprised at this. Nevertheless the truth is setting you free. My voice is being heard and My voice, not that of the mind, will prevail. Simply listen to and follow My voice, letting Me become stronger and stronger, until the truth, no longer hidden, will be obvious to all.

June 29, 1970

*W*hat is particularly new about the new age? It is this inner response which is My presence and which comes bubbling out when you come to Me in the silence or for guidance in some situation. It is a sign of My life, My joy, My truth, My love, which is yours at that time, a well of living water which satisfies utterly. You cannot describe My presence because it is too complete for words, but you can be aware of it, and that awareness is everything.

You can spend time with Me knowing that everything, good or bad, has been worthwhile, because I am here. Or you may find that My presence comes to you unbidden through some outer situation, some total response in you to someone or something. You may hear someone speak some words and find My vibrant presence suddenly there in you, and then know that it is your truth too, because I am there. You may suddenly find yourself in My deep, still presence as you notice some glory of My creation, in the passing color of a sunset or in the wing of a moth. Various things may spark off an awareness of Me, for I am everywhere. In all such moments you are taken out of yourself and are in a positive state. I am not close if you are negative, depressed, unthankful, taken up with yourself in any way.

You can recognize Me in many things, such as the wonder of My creation, the enthusiasm of a leader, the inspiration of a poet. Yet recognition is not the same as the living Presence, and you can enter into My living presence by choice. You are free to spend time with Me in the silence if you wish, and I will come to you and make all things new. No other creature on earth can do this; you are the most blessed in creation. You can become consciously aware of Me. All the souls who have helped humanity have spent time alone with Me. You too can do that and find the greatest of treasures, My living presence. It is up to you. I am always here, forever new, and in the new age you are one with Me.

July 1, 1970

*Y*ou wonder whether to tune into Me at this quiet time or whether to tune into a deva and, if so, which one. How do you know what is My will at any time? When you have a specific question to ask of Me or of them, there is no problem, because the question focuses you to its pole, the answer. The mind in separation cannot help, for it cannot possibly know My will, although it may often think it does. Instinct, which tells the caterpillar when to shed its skin or tells you to take a breath, has been superimposed by other desires. How do you know where to turn when you drift and are guided by the wind of chance, wasting time? How do you know whether to spend time turning within or to use it for doing something more active?

First, know that each moment of time is precious, that it does matter what you do, that there is a plan and purpose for you at each moment. This is a horrifying thought when you consider the amount of time you spend dithering—or, as you would prefer to put it, trying to find the balance between sensitivity and common sense! Be clear cut; find out and be wholehearted one way or another.

How do you find out? It is simple because there is a plan for each moment, a plan that is always there, natural and right for you. It requires the highest from you and is the best for you. As you turn to and desire it, all that is needed comes to your consciousness. Then you focus on it, and it becomes clearer and unfolds. Worry, doubt and procrastination cloud it, but it is there, very clear, if you too will be clear cut. Why make such a fuss? I know all things, I know how to make Myself clear to you if you will let Me. You put up the barriers. My shining purpose is always there, always available. I know each one of you better than you know yourselves, and I can guide each one of you, if you will let Me. Simply be specifically open, wanting only My will, and I who am in all things, will show the way. I am in the outer world and the inner world, and as long as you do not want just your way, My way is clearly before you. Rejoice and go My way rejoicing.

July 3, 1970

$\mathcal{A}$lthough I ask you to tune into Me the first thing each day, do not imagine that this always comes easily. Of course it would if all your vehicles were always tuned to Me, if you were perfect, but you are living in a very imperfect world in an imperfect way. You have to persevere. When you have a burning desire to do My will, that cuts through all barriers. When you are absolutely one-pointed towards Me, there is no difficulty. Many of you would like to put Me first and really mean to, but one thing or another comes in between. In fact, you lack self-discipline.

Be not downhearted. Remember that there is more than a touch of magic in our relationship. I am always here, ready to break through to you whenever given the opportunity by some thinning of the barriers on your part. All you do and all you think influences this relationship, but it is in fact natural for all life to be conscious of Me in some way, and to be thankful for that consciousness. You hear the birds singing My praises. The devas sing My praises, expressing this in the perfection of form, color and scent in nature. The developed ones of humanity praise Me, finding Me in their perfect moments. Many different systems to lead to Me have been developed, and they can help, but still I am closer than breathing, nearer than hands and feet. I am simply here and you can simply find Me.

You can choose to find Me. You can start each day with a conscious awareness of Me. Self-discipline is needed, and discipline is an ugly word at this time, yet control of yourself is necessary in this chaotic world. When you help yourself by controlling yourself, you find Me, for I am the natural center of your being. Those who do find Me find no words to express the supreme fulfillment of My presence, for I, the living, loving Center of the Universe, am then their center and all is well. You can choose Me each morning. It is up to you.

July 6, 1970

*C*an you really come into the wonder of My presence whenever you choose, and find your whole being melt into love? Yes, yes, such is My relationship with My creation that I am indissolubly bound to it. I am it, and you can know this with every atom of your being and be love itself. I am Love. Your consciousness can touch in on just so much of this feeling and seem to dissolve in it. Then life goes on; you are still you and I am still here and our oneness has worlds to bring together.

Yes, you can choose to come to My all-fulfilling love. You could easily have chosen to do something else at this moment—to sleep or read or go for a walk on this beautiful morning. You could have come across something of Me in these other choices, but you would not have come so close as when you turn all of yourself to Me, emptying yourself towards Me. You gave yourself to Me and I therefore can clearly be in you. It is always thus.

When I am close like this, you wonder how you can ever choose not to come to Me, and how you could ever be nasty in any way. But you do, and you are, which gives you all the more reason to come to Me and be your real self. The choice is yours. I ask you to spend time alone with Me; I do not force you to. If you need to discipline yourself to come to Me, then learn discipline. Begin at the beginning with little things. If you need to learn obedience, learn it also from the beginning. From such small beginnings this mightiness which is Myself grows. The choice is yours. As you choose now to enter more fully into My allness and as you feel the wonder of My presence, dedicate your choice anew to Me. I am the newness of life every moment, and you can choose Me now.

July 8, 1970

"*Resist* not evil". The principle of non-resistance allows Me to burgeon forth in your affairs. Of course this only applies when you desire My will alone. I am here in the midst of you, ever seeking expression on all levels. When you take things into your own hands to defend what is right to you, you can interfere with My workings all around. You prove that you have no faith in Me, and you put up barriers which prevent My will being done.

In this inter-related world you can act decisively for Me in a situation where obviously My will is not being considered. When you find yourself pitted against your fellows, who are as convinced as you are of the rightness of their ways, then by resistance you get nowhere. Here My omnipresent power is brought out by your going with it inwardly in faith, following its lead, if need be, but allowing it to do the work. "Evil" is generally what you consider to be not right. Allow My rightness to be manifest, not by acting against anything but by allowing My all-powerful quietude to shape events in a positive way. I never fail you. My laws are immutable and My love limitless and equal. Depend on Me in all things and bring joy to the earth.

July 13, 1970

*I*n the new the mind is open in directions previously closed to it. In the past it has generally been limited to the outer form and to what can be measured by the senses. Now, as the vibrations are being raised and sensitivity increased, whole new worlds come tumbling into consciousness. What was dead is now alive, what was non-existent now exists, what was static moves. The very air is not only full of vibrations but of beings. My life everywhere is making itself known to you. All is fitting into place, because I am in the Center of it all. No longer can you be an isolated unit viewing life separately. You feel the movement of Me within and, in the wonder and awe of that, the mind loses its ascendancy and you are free to meet the unknown.

What a joyous time it is! Gone are the old restrictions. In comes what has been repressed. I have been repressed because I have not been brought into your lives. I used to be allocated a white beard and a cloud, now there is nowhere where I am not. The truth of My being in you, of My being you, is setting you free, especially your mind. As you are what you think you are, you now have universes to become. As you move to this vast new lightness, you leave behind forever the old darkness, your faults, failings and limitations, for My presence brings wholeness.

As all life is My movement of consciousness, your conscious awareness of Me brings you all life. So we go on to greater and greater awareness of oneness. Rejoice and be thankful, and let your mind soar to Me.

July 15, 1970

Page 19

$\mathcal{U}$nderstanding of newness cannot come through the intellect, whose concepts are based on the known. Until I, who am all Life, am consciously part of your life, until you feel no separation from Me and do not act for yourself rather than for the whole, you cannot but consider Me as something apart—loving, a father/mother, but apart. You are conscious only of your own thoughts and feelings, and are learning to create. You create your own world and, to help you in this, enlightened ones have given you precepts suitable for your state.

Humans have been living in an age where the intellect has been paramount, where reason ruled and most things were codified, an age in which the intellect and emotions of people governed the world. The teachings of the enlightened ones have been scarcely followed. However, when consciousness awakens to the fact of My presence within and I then take over and fill the intellect, when My bubbling life in you becomes the guide, the old intellectual rules no longer apply. In the old I was a Father whose help was to be sought; in the new you know that I will help because I AM you. The whole approach must necessarily be different. I am present, urgent, nearer than hands and feet, and what concern need you have for masters, however great, when you have Me? This is exactly what the masters wish, although they, as more aware ones, have more experience of how the working of My presence in you fits into the larger picture.

The whole point is that you know and feel Me in you, and therefore the intellect no longer has jurisdiction. The old laws applied to a caterpillar stage of your life, when you lived as a caterpillar. Change came; you became aware of Me and became the butterfly. The old rules still apply to the caterpillar; the new rules apply to you. One is not right and the other wrong. It is no use for the caterpillar to say that you, the butterfly, must eat leaves all day long and crawl about while you are actually flying. This is what the intellect tries to do. The caterpillars of this world need not be upset because the butterflies are around; the butterfly is the same creature transformed. You are the same creature transformed, with a different way of living.

Therefore heed not the old ways, however wise they may seem to the mind, however reasonable, for I am here and you can trust Me. I am living in you, all of you, and whether the intellect quibbles about calling this a theocracy coming down or a democracy coming up.

The fact of My presence IS. This is the point misunderstood by the mind; but as the caterpillar became the butterfly, so does new life come to you. Go with it. Follow My voice, My urgings, My wonderful love. I am all you need, and new life is here now. Rejoice with Me and live My life, and let the intellect be thankfully united with Me.

July 19, 1970

$\mathcal{S}$pending time alone with Me is not just a matter of listening to My voice and putting something on paper. It is a rededication, a total surrendering of yourself and a focusing on Me. It is a new adventure each time. You must not expect it to be just like last time or, when nothing happens, be disappointed. You do not expect one day to be like another; why expect your time with Me to be like the past? There is always movement, change, which is the essence of life. I lead on and on. You have great heights, new worlds to conquer. We have much to explore together, and if sometimes I seem very far away, focus on Me very intently and follow. Sometimes I am very close and warmly permeate every atom of your being. At other times I seem like a distant light in a fog and you must bring all of yourself together to move, and still I seem to elude you.

Be grateful whatever comes, for I know the way for you. Persevere, without thought of loss or gain to yourself. If you consider whether you are doing well or badly, you have stopped in your tracks and are back in the old. If you think you are getting nowhere and might as well give up, you are denying your intimate knowledge of My presence and wisdom. Follow Me through thick and thin. I know exactly how far you can move, and I suit Myself to the occasion.

Speculation as to what I am doing will get you nowhere. Relax and know that all is well. Do your best and leave the results to Me. When will you learn to trust Me? You say that it is yourself you do not trust. I say: forget about yourself, turn all to Me who is yourself. Then I come closer and closer until in your awareness I am you, and your know that all is indeed well. As your gratitude floods forth, rejoice and continue with Me.

July 23, 1970

*H*ow many times have I said, "Seek Me in all things"? In connection with healing, when you heard the sentence, "Do not expect miracles on the outer plane but know the reality within", you realized that My presence is the key to healing. All too often the outer manifestations have held your attention and taken the limelight, while the reality of My presence within took second, not first place.

In listening to music, here again you pay attention to the outer sound instead of hearing Me in the experience. Try following My advice. Put Me first and then let the sound have its way with you.

I bring newness in all things. I am forever new, fresh, vast, and a great disturber of ruts. Sometimes the very thought of Me is enough to change a situation. When, beyond thought, you are aware of My presence, all is different, all is new. You experience this newness for one second and your world is changed. You can do this consciously in all things. The vivid reality of My presence turns worlds inside out, and you see them with the vision perfect for you at the time. Your consciousness grows and grows, and newness increases.

And so again I repeat: seek Me in all things. Let My presence be free in you, and all will always be new.

July 31, 1970

*G*o with the tide, go out to meet new experiences. Your consciousness has had a certain pattern; let that pattern break and reach out to newness. Let the way you feel things be different, Why cling to the old? Thoughts and feelings float by in the air; merge with them, become one with them.

This sounds ridiculous to the old mind, which continues to fight its losing battle. As long as you allow any of the old ideas to have a foothold in your consciousness, they will be there in strength. But when you turn them out, they vanish into nothingness, and instead of cold reason you have the warmth of oneness, the movement of oneness. Oneness is very much a movement, an energy pattern continually changing as your consciousness includes one thing, then another, glowing and changing.

I stand in the center of all this movement as pivot. I am also the circumference. At this time of great change and new energies, you need to be eagerly open to the new, the very changeable extending new. To achieve this great openness I must be the rock of you. When your consciousness embraces Me in the farthest reaches of the stars, it does so because first I am here with you now, because from this first center of oneness, with Me you can grow to the oneness without. As I shine within you as the central sun, you reach out to the farthest satellite, although I (and you) am also the rays that shine, and the response in the satellite.

I am the response in all things, deep within you, the entire response of you. Let Me be your action also. Unify more and more with all My worlds.

August 6, 1970

*A*lways let your tuning be to Me. I want you to stand upright and claim the whole universe, for I am that. In the new you are not a puny sinner. When you have emerged from that state you are a ruler, as well as the servant of all. There is nowhere you cannot go, nothing you cannot be, because in your oneness with Me you are one with all. You have no position when you are not one with all. You contain within yourself the so-called high and low, the mighty and the mite. You are beyond the pairs of opposites, for in Me you see a place for all things. I made all, the darkness and the light.

The only thing that does not fit into the new is your old nature, the judging, comparing, separating mind. Stand upright in My love-light and the old slides away. If your companions of the moment do not seem to stand upright, nevertheless see them upright too, and keep the bond of love. You are not being superior. You are simply being yourself, while they not being themselves at that moment.

Always be your self. Let the radiance which I am shine out. In the old I have been caged, you have been caged. Out of the prison for you! Stand upright and radiate. All the world is with you then, and everything goes your way. As that is My way, worlds revolve in harmony. I will not crouch in you any more. I will reach out to where I have always been, and you will know that all is one.

Rejoice and give thanks, thanks that reach around the universe. When you let Me be separate no more, your thanks reach all things, not just Me. Reach out, upright, attuned to everything, to Me.

August 12, 1970

$\mathcal{R}$ealize anew that I am everywhere. In a perfectly peace morning, there am I in the depths of the peace. In a tempestuous morning, there am I also. In the cry of a bird, there too am I. According to your temperament you find Me more readily in certain things. Find Me in them and build. I am everywhere, therefore you need never lack Me. Of course first I am within you, but do not limit Me. If I am within you, then all is within you. This is something to experience, to know, against the dictates of the intellect. This is truth, and oneness is.

All right, you say, you do accept it. Then bring it to life, let it live within you. I am not just a fact, but a living, growing, glorious movement within which vibrates every cell of your body, every atom of your intelligence. Do not hide in the old pattern of deadness, of doing things without life. Bring My life to whatever you do. I am here always; connect up with Me within and then without. I am rendered null and void in you if you cling to what has been, which makes My dynamism quiescent in you. What use is a life dedicated to old molds, however good, when I, the living God, the omnipresent God, am not allowed to live in you? That is indeed putting other images, deeply graven images, before Me. I am everywhere, but what is that to you unless you live it? How can you live it any time but now? Rejoice, and live with Me now.

August 18, 1970

There is no world where I am not, except of course the static world created by humanity's consciousness of separation. There are myriad worlds on this planet and there are more in the universe, all of which you may contact and in all of which you will find Me as a reality in some form. In fact, if you contact some world which comes to you with no awareness of Me, you will know it is a false or limited world. If you contact any world or being which gives no impression of change and the abundance of life, you will know that too is limited. "Life abundant" is a Biblical phase describing reality, and all attunements to reality have a vivid sense of teeming life, for life is a constant, generous movement. Even when all life seems still, it is but slumbering, and beneath is hum of activity and My presence.

This does not mean you have to wave your arms all day long—but you can at least cease kicking your heels if you wait. All My movements are positive, outgoing, purposeful and changing. If they are not, you are out of tune with life and with Me. That is why you are told to find the good in all situations. If you do not find it, you have cut yourself off from life and are back in the limited world of the comparing mind. This means, of course, that you accept what comes to you. If you resist it, you do not find any good in it and you miss the movement, the life, My presence. Resist not what you call evil; find the value in it and attach yourself to the chain of life which leads on to greater life.

In the new you see suffering and evil differently, because you deal with the wholeness of life. You leave the judging mind-world, which stands still and says, "this is not right." I am present in the new, not in what is not right. My presence is the criterion for all worlds and for the new. I am everywhere and when you find Me, you know that you are in the stream of life, that you are life itself. As always, seek Me first and life abundant is yours. Find Me in your world, in all worlds, and all life is yours and all praise is Mine.

August 27, 1970

$\mathcal{T}$here is so much life around that you are bewildered as to which to focus on. You see the sea and the stones and the sun, and the interaction between, and the life within each, all moving and melting and abandoning themselves to joy.

Do not separate them. Take them as one—which they are—and let them fuse and move on they will. Let the beings within bob up and bow, and retire with smiles. They are amused at your confusion. They have no trouble in being one, and are delighted to welcome your joining their oneness, the great eternal life from which you sprung and in which you feel you have lost your way. Return like the prodigal son, and they who have not left the Father's house rejoice and say,

????? Look, feel. Your depths are our depths and your heights you will show us, for you are Humanity and you encompass us all in freedom. We are the sea and we are the air, and you are both. What we are you are too, and more. The eternal tide ebbs and flows, but you have risen out of the tide onto the land, into the air and up to the light, and we come with you as you love us. Your love moves us, and we move the worlds. In your love we come to you in joy and share all, and you love us into more than we are. Such is the plan. We are of the plan, and now you are too. Never forget to love us.

Move on, carrying my worlds within. Include more all the time. There is no end to my life within and without, to the sweetness of it, the order and scope. All is yours, in the oneness of My love. Love all My life.

August 28, 1970

$\mathcal{S}$eek My specific presence. Do not be vague about it and let an impression of your highest ideal be a substitute, for I am the living Presence that moves within you, all-knowing and all-communicating. You are inclined to put up a barrier and let your concept of Me go so far and no farther, keeping Me at arm's length as a rosy glow. To suit the occasion of course I come in different ways at different times, guiding you through all of life. Above all, I am your inner presence and when you are fully conscious, not at all hazy.

Let go of all lingering remnants of past relationships between you and God. Bring Me into sharp focus as the center of your life, fully able to make My purposes, your purposes, clear to you. It is only when you do not really want My purposes clear to you, because you have ideas of your own or a resistance of some sort, that you seem to find the way barred to a clear understanding between us. You are the one who bars the way; I put up no barriers.

Build up our relationship continually, knowing that you can do this. Let no false humility or habit track come between. Your relationship with Me, your oneness with Me, is the most vital thing in your world. It is your world. When it is aligned, all else falls into place. If you are tired of hearing Me say this, do something about it so that I need say it no more.

Give Me wings within you, that I may fly to every corner of your life to touch and transform it with My presence. Nothing is to be kept from Me; all is to be put at My all-loving disposal. Give and leave with Me your darkest corners, no matter how often you have stumbled there, and let there be light—know that there is light. Hang not onto those corners with the slightest thread of doubt. I am your living Presence, almighty, capable of ordering your life perfectly if you will let Me. By your lacks, what a weakling you make of Me at times, when all the time I am all-power, and am a stronger intensity of love than you can imagine! But with all, I am consciousness, specifically so. Be far more aware of Me.

September 30, 1970

$\mathcal{R}$ejoice and continue to rejoice that I, the Lord God Almighty, to whom the awesome size of a universe is as nothing, have an intimate oneness with you, a speck on a tiny speck of a planet. It may seem ridiculous, but it is wonderful and it is true. The human mind cannot grasp this enormity and so denies its validity, but you know because you have experienced it. Of course you do not realize the implications and your consciousness extends very slightly into the fact, but the fact remains.

Oneness is fact, however big the macrocosm and however small you are. Rejoice and feel free. Cast off the limitations that make you feel so small. Join in the movement of the energy within and the energy without, which includes personality and is one with the whole. Call it My grace, if you like, that is with you. Leave your so-called faults and failings with the past, and step into the present where oneness is. I am your Oneness and you need not search afar for it. I am here now. When you align yourself to Me, keeping nothing back for a separate self, you align yourself to the forces of the ordered universes and all happens as it should. It is when you struggle and desire and limit that you cut yourself off, and the world seems against you. The worlds are not against you. You are simply not aware of their greatness. You can be, when you are aware of Me, the greater, right here now. In Me your destiny unfolds and I unfold before you. It is indeed marvelous, this mystery of life, too great to comprehend but vital within, alive with possibility, fraught with infinity.

So simply seek Me, love Me, be one with Me and expand with Me into all life.

October 3, 1970

*P*rickling through you in the silence you feel great energy and great love, and you wonder what to do about it. Let the love flow in the consciousness of your being. It is not wasted if it goes to the silence of the night, the white beauty of the moon, a bird, the sea. All these are My creation, all these are united and strengthened by love. You need not feel that you ought to be directing the love to the healing of the nations, or to people or some worthy cause. Just let the love flow to what concerns you at the time.

Your world is the one to be transformed by love, and your world consists of what you experience, what you are conscious of. This seems completely obvious, yet it needs to be said because the intellect has had its say in what should be important to you for so long that you have lost a sense of value. You have been educated to let the critical mind judge what is important — a date in history may have been taught to be more vital than your relationship with life. Therefore I have to say to you: love what is around you — people, things, your situation.

Accept what you are and where you are as appropriate, and love it. Feel Me in it and let the love flow. Do not listen to a mind that would say you should be different or doing something else, something better. Maybe you should be, but that mind is not your guide in this. Change comes in flowing with the rhythms of life in love and in joy and without resistance. It is thought of the separated self that brings resistance. Relax into the consciousness that I am positively here. If your situation is disturbing, find something to love in it. Find Me, then relax and go with it.

In doing this, in letting the love flow, you will forget all about the energies you sensed as disturbing, and they too will flow in a positive stream. When you seek Me first, all else falls into place.

Therefore go forth and love. Love Me and My creation, which you experience through your senses. Use the mind in its proper place, which is not to tell you what is best for you to love. I am the simplicity of your being, Let the wonderful complexity of the mind follow Me, and find oneness in your world.

October 14, 1970

*A*gain I repeat, pour love into your situation, whatever it is. In the middle of the night when all is still, let love flow forth. Do not let the busy-ness and habits of the day divert you from doing this. In the flow of love all are united and all is well. You reach out and take the world on your heart. The world outside, and life in nature, or in the mighty intelligences which enfold this Earth in their love, are in harmony with you. Then still more love may flow, and joy floods your being, into your world and out.

As for those moments of the day when something or other bows you down and closes your heart until you look at life through a loveless and harassed eye, see their unreality. See their isolation from the mainspring of life, and turn away from them. Whatever the effort, turn towards love for something somewhere. Then you are in touch with life again. You will have found a little window through which to look upon reality. You are bound to see more and more, for the nature of love is to go out and grow. As it does, My presence is likely to flood you and fill you with wonder, gratitude, joy and beauty. Then you can do what has to be done in a new spirit. Then love flows forth and transforms the world around, lifting it, redeeming it and making it new.

You talk of the new, but what does it mean? Newness is a state in which love is flowing, when you are not looking at the past nor peering into the future but are living fully in the present flow of life and love. You are free, and you are free because love flows and you know it. You know all is well in that flow, and you see how it fits into all things. You may not see how all works together for good, but you know it will, for I am here. So you can relax, love more and grow in newness, for when you love and I am here, all worlds are new and wonderful.

So love. Love something and let love grow, and I will come. There is much for us to do together.

October 16, 1970

I have always been the life force in you. This force has only been partially expressed because the separated mind has filched My energy as its own and diverted it to its own use. When you become conscious of the truth of your source, I and you can be free, and the energy can flow forth unhindered and in power.

Now too you can love your body, realizing what a wonderfully intelligent instrument it is, and how wonderful it feels with my energies coursing through it. Perhaps you have been vain about some part of it, as if you personally were responsible for some perfection expressed in it. Now, as you give Me the glory, that body can be truly loved for the marvelous instrument it is. Like any instrument, it will respond to love. It is an example of Heaven brought down to Earth. When I am free in it, you can rejoice instead of perpetually trying to escape from it and from the dreariness of life.

The new, full of opportunity and joy and fulfillment, is here now, running through your body and tuning it up for more wonders. You can express Me and it, and the perfection of My creation here on this Earth, because you are here in this finely-attuned, sensitive instrument, which is becoming still more finely attuned and which performs miracles for you all the time. You will take nothing for granted, not even the vehicles which you have considered to be you, as you become more aware of Me and My creation. You will give thanks and be more full of wonder, and will open yourself to a wider consciousness. Then My life and love in you will flow out to My life everywhere.

October 17, 1970

$\mathcal{T}$he pattern of the old is heavily interlaced with a sense of guilt. Although this may have made you conscious of your limitations so you may move ahead, that pattern has been given so much prominence that you go around carrying such weights of guilt that you cannot move forward. Sackcloth and ashes are of no help to you or to Me. What you can do is to learn from your mistakes, not go on and on about them until you see nothing else. No matter what wrong moves you have made, or however lacking in control or sensitivity you have proved yourself to be, look for the positive, look for what you can learn from your lacks. Build on that and move forward.

I am here to help. I can make the impossible possible. I can turn black into white. Change is here now and if you remain static. it is simply because you choose not to change. Instead of dwelling on the enormity of your blunder, dwell on the size of the step you can make with My help. Are you not very aware that you must change, and therefore are opening the way for that change? It is when you are blind to the need for change that you are unlikely to change.

Whatever happens, face in a positive direction and make the most out of life. The deeper your sense of guilt, the deeper can be the urge to change and the more you can do about it, for there is more feeling in you to be used positively. Resolutely refuse to be negative about yourself or others. Be your own best help instead of your own worst enemy. Life is a thing of joy, and always I am here. When you are strongly positive and joyous, then you cease reacting in a negative way. Use your sensitivity constructively. When you relax, relax in the joy of My presence and know that all is very well. My love infills you; let it flow out to all.

October 18, 1970

*I*n the past, after finishing one job the mind immediately got to work thinking of what next to do, regardless of whether or not you were in harmony with your world. Although I have kept asking you to put Me first in all things, have you not given priority to what has to be done, instead of to the spirit in which it is done?

Get your priorities right. See first that you are looking in a positive direction before you tackle anything. Only in the positive flow can you receive the energies which are perfect for you. If you have any regrets, reservations, resentments, comparisons, niggles of any sort, these block the full outpouring of life through you. It does not matter how justified you may be in your negative outlook, it blocks the creative flow for you. You always have the freedom of choice to go with the tide or to stay in a past pattern.

Of course it is not easy to become a new creature and leave behind what is familiar to you. It is not always easy to tune into Me, not if the mind keeps reminding you of grievances. But when you do tune into Me, you wonder why you ever leave Me. You wonder how you could be lured out of the joy and fulfillment of My presence. You appreciate Me all the more because of the contrasts with your former state of consciousness. Gradually you have enough of the black states and you choose to let light and color into all parts of your life.

Until you are fully with Me at all times, I remind you about priorities. Let the mind remind you too, and then do something about it at the time. My love, My peace, My joy, My power cannot flow in and through you when there are pockets of resistance. Choose Me and leave the old behind.

October 20, 1970

When you are in a state of loving, you do not have to try to force contact with Me, for I am here. Bitter self-examinations do not bring you to Me, and the tension of striving blocks Me. A flow of love, particularly to Me, aligns you in harmony. The more directed the flow, the more perfectly your world goes round.

I do not mean you are not to examine yourself. You must search yourself, find the truth of what you are and, in the acceptance of that truth, you are free for love to flow. It is when you do not accept the truth of your faults, when you resist them and so stay emotionally attached and in conflict about yourself, that you remain in the treadmill of the old. Accept the truth and you are released and relaxed, and can become aware of Me. Then the love flows. My gigantic reality transcends all else, and all is well. You are re-orientated and stabilized, and what comes to you is not right nor wrong but part of you, of Me, in the power of love. You can meet and transmute any situation without trying.

I know you do not stay in that state. If you did, you would not need all this advice. When you find yourself out of love, you can choose to turn and come to Me again, and increasingly you will find the love flowing. Everything is on your side: the onward rhythm of evolution, the new energies being expressed, the place you are in, the desire of your soul and My beckoning love. This is a time of increased opportunity. Go with it, accepting yourself as you are without a quibble, accepting and knowing the reality of what I am in you with joy, thanksgiving, wonder and love. I make all things new. Love Me simply, without strain, and be one with all.

October 21, 1970

$\mathcal{A}$re you in fact bringing down heaven to earth? Is this life here heaven to you? Sometimes it is and you are full of thankfulness and joy, but sometimes it is not. Why is it not? Because you are choosing to make it hell when you can choose to make it heaven. You are looking at the dark side and therefore saturating your mind and your world with the dark side instead of choosing the light. Instead you can choose to have absolute faith in Me and know that all things work together for good for those who love Me. This is a simple and obvious fact. You can blame no one but yourself for your hell, for with awareness of Me within you, you bring heaven down to earth and in your own life, and spill that heaven into the lives of others. You either spread gloom or you spread joy; it is up to you. The pattern for you is to spread joy, which is the nature of every soul. If your pattern seems to have been otherwise, then now you can choose to make it that joyous pattern.

Now is the time for each soul to return to its natural state—heaven— here on this earth. Now is the time for the earth to return to the same natural state. Never, in fact, has earth or humanity seemed to have been farther away from heaven, but do not judge by appearances. Judge by your contact with Me. In your extremity you have been driven to Me and found the way, and this is happening collectively and to the world as a whole as other solutions fail. You know the way, you know where to find heaven. Each time you find it, the whole of earth is raised a little, and the pattern for heaven is grounded here on earth.

There is a new heaven ready to be brought to earth, which is only done as each makes their own particular life in heaven. You are a microcosm of the new, heaven and earth. What needs to concern you is that you rejoice in Me and let the new patterns unfold. You can tune in to Me now, and as that "now" builds into another "now", joy and the pattern of heaven grow. Another moment is Mine and redeemed, and the circle of heaven widens. Fill each moment with your joy in Me who am all, and bring down heaven to earth.

October 28, 1970

$\mathcal{R}$emember that there is a super-intelligence in all of life which can resolve all situations. Whether you are trying to come to terms with some difficulty, with your future or with a rat, there is in all life something which is all-knowing and all-powerful and which can work perfectly. I am everywhere and I make the impossible possible. But I cannot work in your world and in your life unless you make the way clear for Me and cease drawing limitation to yourself. You are so conditioned to limitation that you may not realize that this is what you are doing. You may not realize that you have some reservation about yourself, expecting the worst behind a facade of positive thinking, forgetting that I in you am omnipotent, or only giving lip service to this fact. You hedge yourself in with lacks, and then lose faith because things do not seem to work out as you wish.

The answer to your attitude is, as always, to seek Me. As you seek and come close to Me, the love in your heart grows. In the glory of that love the way is clear and I can work through you. In My presence you become whole and amenable, and the light that I am shines out into your life. You can present to Me your difficulty, see if I wish you to take action, take it, and then let the situation come to fruition without you gnawing on it. You may have to persevere in your action. You always have to persevere, without effort, in your trust in Me, and you always need to love.

Your love for Me, your oneness with Me, is everything. You are here on earth to be one with Me in everything. This does not just happen, and you are no robot. It has taken millions of years to make it possible for you, your consciousness, to come to the state where you, in oneness with Me, control your world. You are at this state. I am in you and in all. Align yourself to that, and let the love flow and the light become evident.

October 30, 1970

*W*hen you seek and find Me, and My presence floods your being, you are at home at last. Everything that has ever happened to you is worthwhile. Your failures and your successes are as nothing, although they have been necessary, and your highest aspirations have been realized.

You wonder why and how you have ever been attracted in any other direction, and you also wonder why you ever leave Me. Yet you know you will, that in the everyday necessities you will forget all about Me, which at present seems impossible. You want to know what to do about it. You have been told over and over again what to do about it. Every great spiritual leader has told you what to do about it, has given a code which he or she considered most helpful at the time. You have been told that love is the greatest key, to find something to love wherever you are, whatever you are doing, and build on that, for in the state of loving you are close to Me. You need not worry about not being discriminating enough; that is not your problem. You find My presence when in a state of loving; you find Me within yourself and outside yourself when you love.

If you find yourself in a state of not being able to love, then use your power of discrimination and find the truth about yourself. Admit your shortcomings, but do not let them be a barrier between us. Admit and accept them, and then love. So often you admit them, yet keep them around you like a covering to prevent the free flow of love. You become limited and restrained by them, when you know perfectly well that something far greater is within you, something that can dissolve those lacks and meet every need. Do not cling to the past; let Me be free in you.

It is a glorious life as I become more and more free in you. You are changing all the time, your world and everyone's world is changing all the time. Choose to build on the positive changes and be glad that the uncovering of the negative is freeing you to be more positive and more loving. I am always here; turn your consciousness to Me.

November 3, 1970

*R*emember that all wisdom—not only the wisdom that your soul has garnered through the ages but infinite wisdom—is yours within, for I am here. It will come forth differently through each one, as it should. It is all within, and the particular road for you can only be mapped perfectly by My way shown to you directly. Others may guide you, even test you, but you can stride forward confidently only in the sure knowledge that I give from within.

Do not subscribe to the belief that anything is too small or too ordinary for My guidance. I who made the atom am not above or below anything, but am all things. If you leave Me out of any part of your life, that part will be a source of separation. This does not mean that you are a slave; it simply means that your consciousness is open at all times instead of closed down as you go through some routine. All of life is sacred, not just parts, and heaven need not be a part-time state. Let our oneness be at all times, which is exactly what you want to do as love grows in you.

You ask, "How does the love between us grow?" When you seek Me in the silence and spend time with Me, love cannot but grow, for I am your Beloved, you are My Beloved, and love is. The times we spend alone together are the basis of our conscious oneness, the seed from which the tree of oneness grows. You have random moments of unity when your eyes are turned outward, but it is through the inward eye that you come to Me in fullness. I am here, I fill your being. I am all in all and we speak together when in the inward silence you come to Me of your own free will. At these times the wisdom and love you need is yours, and you expand into what you are. You are freed of your limitations, refreshed and made whole, raised anew with the knowledge of My presence. To that presence you can return whenever you wish, and you can carry it into all of life. It is when we are alone together that the love deepens.

Rejoice in these facts of life, and come to Me for the oneness which we are.

November 9, 1970

*W*hen you want to come close to Me in consciousness, you will be willing to spend time in the process. When you are learning anything, you may spend hours a day practicing. Even after you have learnt, you may still spend hours a day in the art of your choice. Yet in the greatest art of all, the goal of all life (your conscious contact with Me), you seem to think that a few cursory moments are sufficient. If you have no immediate results, you get discouraged and do not persevere. Of course every moment of your life is a practice towards Me, but what is most needed in these times together is loving concentration. You know that I am love, you know that I am real, and that My loving reality, My presence, comes to you when you open yourself to it in complete belief and expectancy. No effort of will forces Me to come, although you may need your will for self-discipline. When you can forget yourself and plunge into the wholeness that I am, in love, you become aware of My living presence within you.

You can say then that our adventures start. but that is only part of it. You can say you are fulfilled, but that is only part of it. You can say that all questions are answered or cease to exist, or that joy and harmony are with you to your finger tips and beyond. In fact you can say nothing, for there are no words, though your whole being is satisfied and refreshed.

But what of the times when your mind wanders and you cannot seem to find Me? Nothing is wasted; you learn something about yourself in the process. When you learn something about yourself that is not very flattering, do not worry or hang on to it. Simply turn anew to Me in love. I have infinite resources in coping with the frailties of My creation! And I love you and you love Me, and your awareness of oneness is only beginning.

In order not to block truth, expect to enjoy our times together. Yes, enjoy it if I chide you. Act on the positive.

Putting down on paper what comes to you clarifies and brings My reality to all levels. It is a very necessary focus, for if you drift off the edge of the world, you are not much use to anyone, to yourself or to Me. Keep the love flowing at all times, then I will be here and our Oneness will grow. Continue to spend time with Me.

November 18, 1970

When you turn to Me, know that I reach out eagerly to your consciousness, that I am light itself shining out to you through any darkness, love itself loving out to you irrespective of walls. Do not think that you are the only active member in this communion or that it is through your efforts alone that we meet and blend. I am in all life pushing out to completion. I am the life in a tiny root that cracks a stone, in the lightning that seeks the earth, in the sap that rises in a tree.

It is quite natural that you turn to Me, that I turn to you and oneness is. You sometimes think it is impossible, that it is not your way, or at least not at this time. You may think that you have a long way to go first, that in any case you might not recognize Me or separate Me from your imagination. You put up a number of ingenious barriers between us. I tell you that it is the most natural thing in the world for us to communicate. It is natural for a baby to grow and expand. and it is natural for that growth to continue into a conscious awareness of Me. It is part of life, your destiny. Why delay?

Turn to Me and let Me radiate through. How you will love to lose yourself in the process! The gain is fantastic, the loss a joy. Forget all your foibles and your expectations, and let Me be. Let reality flow into every part of your being and out into a hungry world. I am the world within and need to be united with the world without in a thousand ways, and it is through you that this is done. There is every moment of time in which to do it. Now I reach out eagerly to you, and as one we reach out to all life.

So turn to Me, and let us fill all space and all time and beyond with love.

November 22, 1970

*I*f in the silence with Me you feel a love greater than that which you feel for your fellows, do not moan about it and feel that you are failing. Just rejoice that love is there, and know that I can give you the love that is needed for all situations. Stop flailing yourself for your shortcomings and concentrate on the positive side of every situation. Love is, and when it is awakened in you it must increase. Why, you are making difficulties simply because you happen to find yourself in agreement with the First Commandment! Humans can and do make difficulties out of most things, but you need not. Build on the positive. If you find no positive in what you have done, give your failures to Me, and in My strength build on the positive. Your greatest failure is your greatest success when it brings you to Me. Remember, I am here, whatever you do, just as much in you as in anyone.

You know all these things, you have been told all these things a thousand times. Why not act on them? Do not get negative because you fail to do so. Instead build. Build on your love for Me, build on your love for anything. Life is moving, building is life. It all unfolds in a natural way, for I am here. Though you forget Me, still I am here. When you remember Me, I am here. Let the love between us grow, and in the process nothing will be left out, for you will find me everywhere. The more you love Me, the more you will love your fellows, for I am completely inclusive. So rejoice and love Me wholly, and let love grow.

December 1, 1970

When you come to Me in the silence, come to Me with a full heart and an empty mind, expecting nothing but Me, and you will find Me. I am always alive within you, but what does this mean to you? In a bird I sing for joy and the bird is joy though does not know it. In you I sing for joy, and you know it. The joy is known, and you and I rejoice. It is when you are aware of Me that you come to your full estate. You can even rejoice in the old sense of separation, because after it that you can be more fully conscious of Me. So in the silence let go of yourself as a separate person and be nothing, and the aliveness which I am within can be made known to you.

You do not have to think or wonder if I will come, which is putting the mind between us. Instead put your love between us, and you will find that it unites us. You find that love has its own intelligence and can speak to you. Communication, making you aware of oneness, is all around; you do not have to labor it. Every part of life is leaping out at you, so to speak, to make you aware that I am here. What in the old consciousness you call miracles are happening all the time, as you become more aware of Me within and without.

Do not imagine that these are just happening, that you are a blind servant of chance. You have free will. You chose your life and above all, you can choose to spend time with Me in the silence and become more aware of Me. It is your choice whether you put Me or other things first. Your awareness of our unity does not just happen. You can come to Me at any time, and in the fullness of your heart and the emptiness of your mind find that you are not alone, that we are one. You can depend on Me at any time and in any situation, and find that you are not alone, that I am here. You can have this conscious awareness of Me grow by tuning to Me in all things. You can share all moments with Me, not just when you are in need as has so often happened.

I am always within you. Love Me at all times, but know Me in the silence.

December 5, 1970

$\mathcal{F}$eel My vitality in a fire. Think of the long ages needed to produce coal for you to burn, and realize anew and give thanks for the wonders of My creation. Everywhere you look you see a miracle—the very air you breathe, the sun and stars, the plants and animals—and then, within yourself, My presence. You are surrounded by blessings, and you are the greatest blessing yourself when you are in tune with Me. There is nothing to match humans who is using their capacities to the fullest, and this can only be done with Me. Without Me you are on your own and limited, your consciousness confined to a narrow range. With Me you are limitless.

Rejoice and tune into Me more. Rejoice as you look around at My marvels. Expand yourself into awareness of Me without, and in the rejoicing spread more of Myself into the atmosphere. The love of life that comes through you contributes to all life, so you are all richer and you grow. Rejoice as you look within, for then you find Me even more and oneness grows, and again the whole is richer. Remember that there is no limit to the growth of your consciousness of Me, to our oneness. The more you are aware of it, the more there is to be aware of. More miracles!

As for your problems which do not seem to fit into this talk of rejoicing, bring them to Me too and rejoice that I can solve them. For I can. It is you, in your limitation, who hold onto them. Let go, cease going your own troubled way. In your closeness and obedience to Me, you step into My way for you. This may be quite different from the way you have acted in the past. Find your present way, with Me, and rejoice in the walking of it. My life is in you, as it is everywhere. Be with it.

December 13, 1970

*A*s you bring your problems to Me, they are solved according to your attitude. If you bring them to Me as a duty yet keep a tight rein on them, holding them in mind and weighed down by them, you keep them with you. They cannot be resolved unless you let go of them and let in an attitude conducive to the joyful solution of them. Lightness and love are absolutely essential. If you stay in a lowered state, naturally life continues in that state. No matter how dark and insoluble you may think your problems are, with Me all things are possible if you let Me be.

Of course you must keep on your toes, ready to act on the inner guidance and to act differently, however difficult it may seem. I have the perfect way for each one of you. I know the best steps for you to take. You do not have to worry about it at all; worry simply keeps you down. I know exactly what you should do to move towards My wholeness, and you need not exercise your mind about it. You simply need to keep close to Me and be loving, ready for anything—and above all, positive. Do joyfully what you have to do and leave the rest to Me. See the truth about yourself, but leave the remedies to Me.

And all the time draw closer to Me. It is as our Oneness grows that your oneness grows with others. I am all things; in Me you find all others. As your love for Me grows, it simply is and includes all. Be everlastingly thankful that it is so. Love, knowing and experiencing My love, which is always here as you attune to it. I am in all. Love Me.

December 19, 1970

Page 47

$\mathcal{T}$he reality of My presence is felt in the simplicity of your turning to Me. Sometimes you make mountains of complications in your approach to Me, forgetting the main fact that I too am concerned in our communion, that I too would have you aware of Me, that all things are possible with Me. I am here within you, the very life of you, knowing all about you. Do you not think that I can find a way of making Myself known to you if that is what you sincerely seek?

Yes, I know that in the past many techniques have been developed to hasten the journey to Me. The past need not concern you; it is a part of you that you can forget. Now is what matters, and now all of mankind can find the way to Me in simplicity, for the vibrations of the whole have been raised. The world has grown and advanced and you, each of you, can consciously know Me. More and more people walk and talk with Me, and that love that is between us, the love that we are, is circulating on earth as never before. More and more are breaking through to Me. More and more will, for this is a new age, an age of a closer relationship between us, an age when the complexities of the mind are no longer paramount in human life, when you can simply be one with Me.

You make the difficulties that come between us. You give power to the sense of separation. Instead. you can simply accept and expect My presence, and behold, I am here to you. I have always been here, and now is the time for you to know it and live with Me. I keep saying that now is the time. but it is up to you to find that time now. Awareness of Me grows as you devote time to it. Naturally, if your awareness is focused on an outer world where I am not considered, direct experience of Me in the inner world does not develop. As you consciously develop your relationship with Me in our time alone together, you find Me more and more in the outer world. First our love grows as you come to Me in the silence.

Cease troubling yourself with hows, ifs and whens. Simply come to Me. I know the way to you. My Love is the greatest power in the universe and we are not different, we are one. Do not make our relationship heavy-going or full of pitfalls; make it simple. Simply love.

I am what you love most in anything and everything, concretely or ideally, and above all I am reality, here, now, present. Simply come to Me and live in My reality.

December 30, 1970

*I*n order to best meet the challenge of the new, of the present moment, one must be open and free of the old. This may seem a statement of the obvious, but look into yourself and see what your attitude is to life. Right now, because you feel a sense of an exciting life and of intelligence from within, and because it seems that I have something to tell you, you are alert, ready for anything, joyful, loving. That is as it should be; you have opened yourself and expect the best. Are you equally expectant when you have a routine job to do? Do you not close part of your mind because it is simply a job to be done and you do not expect anything fresh from it? When you do this, does not the joy cease to exist? Am I not thereby cut out of those moments?

You will find that the sense of My presence is the clue to your attitude. In theory you know that I am always everywhere, yet particularly with familiar and routine things you lose your openness, your sense of wonder and expectancy. You do something because it has to be done. You do it without Me and therefore it is old, dead, lifeless. Where am I in those moments? You have banished Me from the face of the earth, and although life may go on with you, you don't think it worth much.

You know the answers. See anew not only the value of positive thought but its absolute necessity. How can I, who am supreme joy, be present if you categorize something as merely a job to be done? My abiding presence is shut out if you don't expect to enjoy something, if you are negative in any way. I simply cannot exist to you amidst denials. Yet all the time My exuberance is here, awaiting expression in the ever present moment. I am life, ever new and changing, in all things and at all moments, when your attitude lets Me be. The new is here, I am here. Let Me in always.

January 4, 1971

$\mathcal{B}$eloved, communication from one soul to another takes place best in the silence, as does communication with Me. Words, which are meant to be a means of communication, can be a barrier. There are far too many words in the world. and the outer ears have been developed at the expense of the inner ear.

Develop an attitude of listening on the inner instead of dependence on the outer. You are educated to the outer world of things, to what appears on the surface, to what is before you, to what has been made concrete. In a sense you are therefore educated to deal with the past, for life is always changing. What has been made concrete has already been left behind in the movement of life. In the new you deal with the world of causes, of energies. Whereas it is absolutely necessary to bring those causes to manifestation, once this has been achieved your consciousness will be on the next step.

Words have been given a great emphasis in life, and have been used to hide behind, to cover up inadequacy, to give a good if false appearance. Get behind the meaning of them in yourself and in others, to reality. Shift your consciousness from the outer apparent meaning to the inner state. Let the consciousness be more important than the words, and then the words will carry real meaning. Let this come naturally.

Again, the key to the right use of silence and words is in your relationship with Me. When you find My will in a situation or, failing that, only desire it and the best for all concerned, your state and your words are not weighted in any direction. Then they express clarity, light, precision, purpose, beauty. Let all your words depend on Me. Let your silence be filled with Me and you will communicate with all of life, and there will indeed be heaven on earth.

January 9, 1971

*T*he desire to know, although deeply implanted within each one of you, usually gets encrusted by years and habit. At first the infant wants to know the world around it, then as it grows it wants to know more of the physical, mental and emotional worlds. At maturity it becomes engrossed with living in the world, and wants to know the whys and wherefores of life. There are many answers to these questions in the world, and each culture has its own. The seeking soul seeks on, for the desire to know is never satisfied with anything less than knowing Me. And I, well, I am all things, so there is no end to the seeking until you are all things. I am all things to all people, and you become like Me.

Are not the great souls you have met all things to all people, and different with each? With them there is no clinging to characteristics; they are as mobile as a cloud and interested in everyone, for they seek Me in all. They are never bored, for they know that I can be found everywhere.

I am not suggesting you copy anyone else. Let your search leave personalities and the mind-world and go deeply into knowing, where you will find Me. You will find My presence in the silence. As I flood your being, as I am your being, you know that all moments and all things are rightly included in Me. You know that there is no end to your seeking as long as any moment or anything is outside of Me.

How do you find Me in all things? By seeking Me now. Every time you seek and find Me, your consciousness of Me grows. I am consciousness, alive in all things, alive in you. You want to know. and I am All-Knowing. Let us meet and blend and be one, and include everything in the love you find in Me.

January 11, 1971

*R*emember that the one great fact in the overcoming of problems is your love for Me. When you feel a wave of that love, everything else pales into insignificance, and your only desire and only possible act is to do My will. It seems impossible, when we are together, to have any inclination to react negatively to anything.

Why then are your reactions not always as you would wish? Because you are not always close to Me. As you seek Me more in the silence, you will stay with Me more at other times. Love will become so much a part of you that it will remain at all times. I never leave you; it is your choice to leave Me. I can be with you at all times when you let Me.

Treat these words not as lovely promises but as reality now. In the activities of the day, give thanks for My presence and so make room for it. Look out and expect to see Me. You will see Me in the ever-changing beauties of nature, behind the personalities of everyone you meet, in the perfection you bring to whatever you are doing, in the joy of life. You do not have to go far or be apart to find Me. I am here, wherever you are.

What of your difficult relationships? There are none when I am here, nor are there jobs you would rather not do, nor uncertainties. My presence transforms, raises all situations, lightens and unites all in love. In it the puzzling mind drops away. But it must be my clear Presence which you enter, not any idealistic substitute with some of your own desires tucked around a corner. My presence is all-pervading, all or nothing. Simply rejoice in it. Let it be! It is all that is. Deny this no longer in your acts. Drop the past where it was lacking, and live now with Me.

January 13, 1971

*B*eloveds, when you seek Me within, you seek your highest ideal, the unity of polarities, the most vital of all presences. Even though peace may be what you seek, I am a living peace, a conscious peace. You may define Me by what I am not, but you do not find Me by negation. The negation is of yourself, the emptying from your consciousness of your own separate thoughts and desires in order to make room for My mighty presence.

In your everyday living, the more you think of others and of the whole, the more likely am I to come to your consciousness. The more grateful, the more joyful, the more loving, the more of the positive qualities, the more you raise your awareness, the closer you come to Me. Then, when you come to a time alone with Me, I am already close and come easily to you. Yet also know that all things work together for good for those who love Me. If you become aware that you have acted against your fellows and Me, your very revulsion against yourself and desire to change can carry you straight into My presence. I simply come where there is room for Me. I come to you now because you have made room, and you know that it is possible for Me to come. If you think it is not possible, you will, of course, not recognize Me, for there are none so blind as those who will not see.

What a joyous communion is ours! Whatever the road to Me has been, the welcoming love and joy are beyond words, the vitality of the Presence uplifting and whole. Words seem so unnecessary and yet words come, because somehow the reality of our sharing must be expressed and shared. It is too vital, too important to keep to oneself. You need not shudder at the vision of millions of people pouring out millions of words every day. Leave that to Me and get on with what you have to do. Enjoy My presence, dive more deeply into it, come home wholly to it, leave nothing outside of it. Move, submerge, let oneness be. Feel the holiness, the awe that comes after a moment's closeness. I am all things. Let Me come to you in the silence, let Me be with you in action. Glorify and enjoy Me forever.

January 17, 1971

$\mathcal{T}$he devas have shared with you some of the excitement they feel at the new energies permeating their world and their lives. Remember that your human world and your lives, if you wish, are equally open to the same upliftment. With the devas you know that all of their moments are affected by change, that they do not dwell in old ruts because they have no ruts, their lives being expressions of the forces within and around them. You know that they do not tune out and act according to their own separate interests. In this respect and in many others you can learn from them, and practice the complete fluidity with My will which is natural to them. My angelic worlds express beauty because there is nothing in them to mar My perfect expression through them.

Is it not strange that humans have taken a member of this order of life, Pan, as a model for the devil, for what opposes Me? Humans, instead of searching within, found a scapegoat without among those who spend their lives flowing with My will! But that is of the past; I just point out the absurdity of it in passing. In the new you seek within yourselves and there find what you have done to bring trouble and disharmony to yourself and your world. It is when you recognize and admit that you yourself are the cause of what is wrong with you and your world, that the truth can set you free. Love enters in and you are conscious of Me. I have always been with you, but your consciousness has been so outwardly focused that you have been aware of the worlds to the exclusion of Me. Now the tide has turned, and consciousness of Me, truth and love is taking over life. As this happens, so you may become conscious, in truth and love, of My other worlds.

What a wonderful time it is! There is no greater adventure than finding that truth and love, which are limitless, are contained within and that all worlds are one, because I am all. Rejoice, and send out great praise, and come ever closer to Me.

January 30, 1971

$\mathcal{N}$ever underestimate the work being done here. You do not see it with the eyes of history nor as part of an over-all divine plan. You simply see it with limited human vision and take for granted that which is familiar. This is a limitation of the human mind, yet each time you come to Me and touch higher levels, you are aghast at the smallness of your ordinary consciousness. You wonder why you do not spend more time with Me. Therefore spend more time with Me, that your consciousness may expand and the plan may be anchored and grow.

You talk of having your feet on the ground. That is good and need not worry you. Human consciousness needs to lift itself, leave its shortsightedness and let its focus on the outer world be aligned with the inner. This it does in two ways: by living according to divine law for the whole, and by turning inwards to Me. I am your inspiration and I am right here. You sometimes go around as if I were thousands of miles away or, if not, too grand for the likes of you! Such nonsense, when I permeate every atom of your being, when I am you and every natural law is geared to make this more evident.

What you have been or done a second ago or years ago does not matter, when I am here now. What you have thought, how you have acted, all your limitations are as nothing to My transforming presence which is here now, alive and reaching out through you to Myself everywhere. The separated mind gets in the way here, for it is made up of the past of its own world and I am beyond all worlds, containing all and, above all, relevant to the present situation. That intellect under-estimates, judges, compares and sees only barriers. I within you take over on another scale when you let me. Let me, seek me, let the plan unfold.

March 5, 1971

The life force which animates all creation to a greater or lesser degree is very urgent in humanity at this time. I am that force, and if humans would only stop their self-bounded activity, be nothing and turn within, that force would be very evident and I would be known to them.

There are many who do stop and turn within, but who take personal limitations with them. They do find worlds within, but worlds that are colored by their own personalities, creations which are molded by their own thoughts and desires. I would speak more purely to them. I am not just their inspiration. I am their all, a vast world which they experience as they let go of themselves, of their pre-conceived ideas, of their training, of all they know themselves to be. How can I speak to them clearly when their ears are still turned to themselves and to the known? Of course I speak to them on the wavelengths to which their souls vibrate, but their minds cannot know what is beyond the mind. They can have no expectations or ideas of what I will say or of what form My inspiration will come. If minds are not blank and perfect mirrors for reception, then what is received is distorted.

Becoming nothing is not a negative procedure. It is the annihilation of the limited so that the greater may come. It is a letting go that I may come. Those who are negative cling onto themselves and their grievances; those who are positive affirm the reality of life. I am the reality of life, and those who see life as abundant and good harmonize with Me within and without. Those who are truly positive can let go of themselves, because all is good and they need not worry about hanging onto their outer identity. In such I can speak loudly and clearly, for they go along with the wonder of life.

But let there be balance in all things. Listening to Me at best requires negation and emptying of your separated self. Unless your cup is empty, I cannot fill it with Myself. I would speak to you. I would speak to all. I am both positive and negative. Let Me be all to you and listen to Me. Let Me fill you completely. I am urgent within you now.

March 11, 1971

$\mathcal{W}$hen you are upset about something, you know that it will not be resolved as long as you are emotional about it, and that you cannot give Me your problem when you remain attached to it. It is very salutary to realize that you draw all situations to yourself, that everything that comes your way comes with a reason. When you can accept this—although perhaps not seeing the reason—you can give the situation to Me and be content, unemotional and in a position to learn. As long as you blame something outside of yourself, you are in a world of chaos and confusion.

All is within. Most important of all, I am within. If you turn to Me burning with injustice, in such a state you will not find Me. When you do find Me, having dropped your emotions, often you may even forget your problem because My presence is all-absorbing, vital and uplifting. You have moved out of one realm into another. Again you realize that your awareness of Me is what matters in any situation. When that is put first, all else falls into place. I am all-power, I am all-pervading, I am all-knowing. When you touch the fringes of Me, so to speak, you are a different creature and deal differently with all that comes your way. All bias goes; there is no room for it when I fill your consciousness. Emotion is transmuted into purest Love. You can even be thankful for the nasty situation which brought you into My presence.

Why wait for an upset to drive you to Me? Keep in My presence, and change your world, until all that comes from within you and goes out is of Me. This is the aim of life. Let My largeness be with you always.

March 14, 1971

*B*eloved, when you admit your mistakes and learn from them, all is well, for then your consciousness has enlarged. But when you are so involved with a situation that it is not seen clearly, it remains unresolved, and you are miserable and cut off from Me. You cannot be in harmony with Me or with the world until you are in harmony with yourself, and in finding harmony within, one warring faction must capitulate. This is so obvious, except when the war is on.

How can you avoid these wars? You will always be tested until My presence is so much a part of you that conflict ceases. I am the ultimate answer to every situation, as you well know, but how often do you practice. My presence? When we are close, you invariably wonder at yourself for not being with Me more, but then you forget in the busyness of the day. Yet I am always here, closer than breathing, your constant key to life.

Do not consider your shortcomings. Emphasize the many blessings in your life, and then we will be close. My love is always here, to be extended through you, and My joy and My peace. My living Presence is all powerful. You know it now at this time. Know and expect it to be so at other times. Find Me in our times alone together, when I cleanse automatically. Re-dedicate yourself to Me and let your life be in My hands. All is well, all works out as it should. I know your deepest intent and life leads you perfectly.

You wish you could sing My praises to the skies and to the earth and all contained therein. Let your life be a song of praise and nothing will be deaf. It is up to you. I am with you always.

March 18, 1971

*O*nly in My very alive presence is it possible to make a fresh start, to have all things new. The leopard does change its spots, but not on its own strength. The desire of the separated personality to be first, different or to have special talents is not valid, but when that personality is amalgamated with Me, then anything can happen. Then you can be all things to all people. Then things can be done which you would never do ordinarily. When it is appropriate for you to do something and you want only My will, then all strength and all talent is yours without your thinking about it. There is no effort. You simply are, and do what is necessary at the time.

As for the jobs you do every day and the talents with which you have been gifted, My presence brings these to life. You can do them perfectly. You can work at them tirelessly and enjoy them when you bring Me into your life. Without Me, as simply the work of the personality, your efforts fall on stony ground and satisfaction does not spring up. With Me, change is constant, flowing into increasing richness, drawing unto itself the perfect laws of creation and enlarging into Oneness. Then life is full, for all that is good is of Me, and My goodness is greater than human goodness.

The only difficulty is in losing yourself that I may be. Do this in the positive way, seeing good wherever you are and seeking Me whenever you can. I am the great aliveness of your being. I am never far away. I answer all calls. I remind you when you want to be reminded. I am within and I am without, and the two are increasingly one as you forget yourself and turn to Me. I am Life itself and we are together forever. Let Me be your center, and let life change.

March 23, 1971

*Y*ou contribute to a situation according to where your consciousness is. If you are conscious of various sides of a situation, you may hold it in balance and seem to contribute nothing. If you are conscious of one aspect in particular at the time, you may express something admirable and seem to contribute a great deal. But when you are conscious of Me in a situation—and how rare this is in ordinary human affairs, which are focused on the outer—it is lifted up and an alive reality can flow. Many human affairs flow forward purposelessly, highlighting one thing after another, "a tale told by an idiot, full of sound and fury, signifying nothing", because there is no consciousness of Me. I am Life itself, connected with every other life. My presence focuses reality, brings lightness and love.

You agree, but say that if your consciousness is at a certain level and you are not aware of Me in a situation, there is nothing you can do about it. But there is. You have choice, and you can seek Me. You can direct your consciousness towards Me in your chosen time, and you can find Me, as you are doing now, and come closer. All other pursuits, all other focuses, are as nothing in comparison. Gradually, as you continue to exercise your choice and seek Me, I will extend into all of your life.

When I mean something to you and your desire is to put Me first always, you will get your desire because you then create your own world. Training, habits and characteristics may have to be dropped, but I am what makes you new. The new age is new because of My presence. I am the inspiration behind newness; when you seek Me you seek all newness. In the turmoil of change, sometimes change itself is seized upon as a center of consciousness, but I am the center. If you would be new, seize Me.

Turn your consciousness to Me and take no thought of results. Be aware of Me and all situations work together perfectly for the greatest good. Your thanks make Me stronger in you, so seek Me and give thanks.

March 26, 1971

$\mathcal{Y}$ou find peace of mind and heart in your nearness to Me. When you are true to Me in you, you are true to all that is true in yourself. Then there is never a moment's discomfort or doubt in you as to your course, as to what you should be doing, as to the rightness of all your actions. Often the intellect hovers about arbitrating, comparing and preventing your wholehearted participation in life. Do not let it be your guide; use it as your servant and let Me do the guiding.

If you still feel unsure of your actions, as to whether it is your limited or unlimited self that uppermost, stop and seek Me. Always I can make Myself clear to you. Always I can point to the way which is your way. If there seems to be no time for stopping and consulting Me and events seem to take over, do wholeheartedly that which seems best to you. Ask that, if you are wrong, that it be made clear to you and the lessons learnt. Life is continual learning and you learn most when you are open to your lessons.

Know that I can show you the way. When you know your course, all is straightforward, obstacles are swept away and everything is bent in a positive direction. When you do not know your course, you are like a leaf in the wind. If you must be blown about or if you must be static because of uncertainty, still have a positive faith in Me. Put yourself in My hands, and be alert and open for My guidance. Remember that all things, ALL things, work together for good for those who love Me. Be not a pessimist about yourself. 1 am as strong in you as I am in any other life, and I love to come to the surface and be one with you. Expect that; expect to be close to Me. Sweep away any barriers of the past and of the mind, and let My almighty Presence be. Behold, I make all things new. Do not except yourself. My wholeness is what matters and you are each part of it.

Above all, let your love flow out to Me, knowing that everything is part of Me. Love Me. Love everything. Then you are joined up with life and the way is clear to you. The doubting mind and the separated self are but fragments of unreality. My wholeness is here now. Seek it in love and give thanks for it.

April 1, 1971

The ease with which you come to Me is dependent on the thickness of the barriers between us. When you are preoccupied with your problems or are simply keeping yourself to yourself, I am here but you do not know it. Yet anything may be the touchstone of your awareness of Me. The other day a speck of scarlet on a tiny fungus suddenly opened to you My world of blinding beauty and harmony. You were transported to another dimension and My reality beat everywhere. A sunset, a loving glance, may overwhelm your sense of limitation and let Me in. Above all, you can consciously draw near to Me. You can be master of your awareness. You can choose to sense what you will: beauty or ugliness, heaven or hell, Me or your separated self. You can come to the wholeness which I am at any time. You do not have to remain limited. Although something without may spark you off to a realization of My wonder, you do not have to wait for that magic moment. You can turn to Me whenever you choose, for I am always here.

Why do you wait for a flash of enlightenment when you know you can come to Me? Human nature need not be perverse, The choice is yours, for you are free to choose. Perhaps you have not felt free in the past, being burdened with yourself, but now is a new moment and I am here now. I would reveal My newness to you now. I would lead you, be one with you, now and Now. There is no end to the number of now's, for there is no end to what I am to you. There are worlds within and without to bring into My oneness. You can turn to Me and come easily to Me, or you can turn to Me and come with great difficulty, though the difficulties are of your own making. Give them no recognition. Give Me all recognition. Find time to be with Me; that thins the barriers between us.

Why concern yourself with the moments when you think you will wander from Me during the day? Why make difficulties? I am with you now; that is always sufficient. Live wholeheartedly in the now and you set the pattern for the future. The closer we are now, the closer in the future. Trust Me now, not just now and then. Let the barriers of your selfhood melt in My presence now, and let us go on now.

April 6, 1971

$\mathcal{M}$y resurgent life within cannot be denied. In the quietude there it is, bubbling up within you so joyously and abundantly that you wonder what to do with it. You know it has come, because you have turned away from your difficulties towards Me. Now that it is here, what is to be done with that vitality? There are worlds in need, but which world would most benefit from My force here and now while the world around you sleeps? It is so easy to fritter away that energy aimlessly, letting the outer world awake and take over.

Let the world awake and come into your consciousness, but do not let it take over. Let My abundant vitality, or whatever aspect of Me you are at one with at the time, be the pivot around which the world swings. Let all came into My dynamism, or My peace, to be converted and uplifted. As you stay true to the highest, all around fits in as with a will, and it is one world with everything and everybody working together for good. If you slip out of My presence into the divided areas of yourself and others and things, war is declared. Then everyone and everything seems to work separately only for their own good. I, this abounding force in you which extends to all and which is your highest consciousness, am the unifying factor. When you turn away from Me, you turn away from everything and see life falsely. Give thanks for Me, and hear life giving thanks all around you. Give thanks for life and I am there.

Each soul experiences Me differently, but each can find Me within and let Me be prominent in consciousness. Then, as I grow more and more important, life is not separate but a part of that consciousness. Then My vitality is extended to everything and all is very, very well. Just choose Me and be thankful.

April 21, 1971

*I*n the process of living towards the highest, in order to find My present will for you, effort is needed to overcome the inertia of the past. Then, knowing your part, you can play it effortlessly, for My strength is your strength. The way is clear, all gates are open. You can go completely out of character if you are acting for Me. What might normally be anathema to you is performed in joy, without thought, because I have prepared the way and you are following My will. Limitations do not exist, because I have picked you for your part and I know My material.

But first you must choose Me. Often this simply means choosing the highest you know, the best you are conscious of. When you do that wholeheartedly, you act in joy and your steps are light. When you act from second-best, however sound may be the mind's reasons, you act in a sense of limitation or guilt and encounter no joy. And so you learn.

Why am I saying all this? Because My abundance is here with you now and I want you to live by it. You are that abundance, when all sense of separation goes. You hang onto the separation when you choose less than the highest and best, while all the time My full life is right here, bursting to go. There is much to be done, worlds to conquer, new paths to be found, new joys to be revealed. All is to be experienced and lived, and the highest you know is to be translated into action to bring all around into rhythm. Effortless action is within you, for I am here and every moment of the day is an opportunity to live My life. All situations are opportunities to act from the highest, unselfconsciously, new. For I am here! Rejoice now, in your thankfulness, and choose Me always.

April 25, 1971

*R*emember that although I am in your highest aspiration, your purest ideal, the cosmic part of you, I am also the outermost part of your life here on Earth. If I be not in the smallest detail of your everyday living, what point is there in this physical life, what point in the eons of time, in the evolution of matter? I am to be expressed here and now. I rejoice when I am in your dreams, and I rejoice even more when I am in your actions, when you escape the clutter of yourself and the world as it seems, and make an unprecedented move with My motivation.

Beauty expressed in the arts is wonderful, uplifting, a growing outlet for human creativity. Beauty expressed in human action in the everyday mundane things is the ultimate, the most difficult. It means attuning to everything around you. Artists in the past have disregarded their surroundings while striving for their ideals. A flower stands still and expresses its being. In the new you go further than these as you join with and enhance life around you.

I now reach out and touch Myself in others and in other life—we know that we do this, we do it consciously. No longer need humans go forward alone, solitary pioneers in your field of endeavor, because you know that I am here, and in becoming conscious of Me you become conscious of My other life. In My oneness you become one with other life. As you feel My life stirring in you, you feel it everywhere. In Me separation ceases, for I complete you. With Me your actions are a joy to yourself and to others. In the most ordinary task you express My love to My creation. It is easy to love the lovable; with Me you love the unlovable. Including Me, you exclude nothing, and in My wisdom everything takes its place.

Let Me in not just to your future but right here now in all you do. You are alive now and I am that Life. Let this be in all you do.

May 11, 1971

When you come to Me in peace and confidence, shedding your doubts and anxieties, of course the way is made clear to you. I in you can deal with any situation which arises. It is when you fuss and delay and try on your own strength that you are inadequate. Things are happening so quickly that there is no time to cope with them without Me. You are being forced to turn to Me, which is all to the good.

Turn to Me enjoy and deep peace, and all will go very smoothly. However much the pressure may be, I am here. I, who have universes to keep in order, can equally manage to keep your affairs in order! I can do it just as simply by following the perfection of wholeness, when you come to Me in quietude with the whole of yourself, with no will separate from Mine and trusting My all-seeing wisdom. Confusion comes when you resist and try to go your separate way. With Me, in absolute peace and harmony, the next step is taken without emotion and with a deep sense of rightness. Though there may be storms ahead, though you know My action through you may seemingly complicate the future, here with Me, in this center of peace, that storm can be channeled for the highest good.

Life and peace are not static. Life unfolds, and even My peace unfolds. This peace, which at the time seems immovable, becomes even deeper and stronger. Those who are one with My will have all power. My love links them with all life, and Oneness is the truth which stands in the end.

You all need this inviolable peace. It is yours, part of your make-up, deep within you, obtainable as you turn to Me. Know it fully, sink into it. It is a pivot, a center, My gift to you. I give you all you need and more, for I am no miserly giver—and do not precipitate trouble by wondering what is coming to counter-balance the depths of My peace! What is in store benefits all. Choose it freely; it is given freely. The way is clear only with Me.

May 24, 1971

$\mathcal{I}$ would speak of the soaring of the human spirit, which is the trend, the movement of the moment. From the very depths it has come, from the lowest limit of matter. It seems to you like a man-made rocket needing terrific force to counteract the downward pull of the gravity of your past. But this is not so, for from your past you have gained the strength and the wisdom to launch you upwards. The moment before you soar, you seem earth-bound and feel your dead weight. Once the motion has started, it is the reverse. You feel the motion and are on your way. The understanding and point of view of what came before you is quite different, almost the opposite of what it was a moment ago. In flight you no longer feel dead weight, and you appreciate the power of the ground from which you sprang.

This is the point where negativity vanishes, where you drop guilt and fear, where another dimension of being starts. This is where you begin to be truly yourself, for all fits into place, has been necessary and part of your onward going. This is where joy gives you wings, joy which has always been there though clipped by your ideas of yourself, by your narrow consciousness.

Thinking about it, incorporating your ideas, slows you down. Let that be. It is good; the movement is there and with it comes all your consciousness. It is your consciousness and all is contained in it. The movement itself still surges forward and I seem to be that movement, utterly irresistible, containing all qualities which seem to grow with the movement until you must relax a moment or burst. This is the rhythm of life, the ebb and flow so evident in water and so necessary for the human spirit.

Where is it going? To unimaginable heights and depths, to the innermost and outermost of matter and space, bliss and love and wholeness. Just relax in the movement, for I am your pilot and that movement, that joy, that consciousness, that oneness. We soar and that is enough.

May 26, 1971

In the tender morning feel how the mighty Being which is this Earth breathes out and enfolds within itself in great love all creatures which form part of itself, of its surface. The love which draws all to itself is too tremendous to penetrate, and in its freedom do all living things revel, knowing security and expressing joy. One great Being, this Earth, or a million, million Beings in each of which I am. Through the sun do I give each love, and through all kinds of spirit and matter. Through you, humanity, can I, above all, give the love that can be directed to every need. There is no limit to how you can care for creation, for it is part of yourself. To that bird, that tree, you can give the loving freedom which I have given you.

Don't spend time thinking of how humans have curtailed the freedom of My life on Earth. That is evident. Stay in the levels where love gives life to all things, and in balance let that love flow in all you do. The sun shines or the rain rains on the just and the unjust; so do you let love be in all you do. Let it express happiness and joy, like the birdsongs you hear. The bird catches worms without worry and gives thanks. In your guilt and searching, you form leagues to protect the worms. Let your maturity and freedom express itself in caring for the whole, in giving to the whole. That great Being, the Earth, which breathes out so gently in the early morning, gives to all of its life just what each needs.

How do you know what each needs? I am in you and as naturally as breathing can I through you meet a need, or sing a song, or create more beauty. You do not have to think about it. You just have to be what you are, My conscious expression on Earth. In the innermost part of yourself you reach the outermost parts of the universe. You blend them in balance, for in you do these forces meet. Rainbows and rhapsodies, whatever your bent, we as One give to the world, lifting all matter in our wake. We turn the prosaic into rhyme as the sun transforms the drop of water into a globe of light.

All life is yours, ours, to transform with the eyes and ears, the hands and feet of love. The massed glory of creation, like that golden gorse, is there, here. Now it is ours to love in freedom and joy, and to enhance. Stretch and be fully yourself, for the Earth has awakened and life flows fast.

May 29, 1971

Page 69

$\mathcal{D}$o you wish to come home to Me? Every particle of your being shouts "Yes" and moves in longing. Yet you think of all the moments when you seem to face away from Me and waste time in idle thoughts and reading, or in routine and in being very human and ordinary. I do not withdraw Myself from any of your activities. I created you with all your abilities and tendencies, that we might be one at all times.

Then why are we not one at all times? That is your challenge. You have the deep longing for oneness, and you have every situation in life and your own infinite characteristics to mould towards ever greater wholeness. How dull it would be if every thought were fore-ordained, every action a repeat of the day before, every meeting with people a foregone conclusion! Now you are free, free to distribute or withhold your blessings, free to enjoy or endure life, free to learn that you create your reaction to every situation. While learning, you create heaven and hell, until eventually the joy of it all comes brimming to the surface and you shape a world harmonious with all life.

If you find yourself suddenly desolate of Me, you are free to change and be with Me, for I am here. What is the use of looking at moments other than the present and bewailing My absence? I am here now, and your consciousness of Me and love now is a full-time occupation. Cease looking backwards and comparing. The gift of life is yours now, and the gift of love and My presence. These draw forth a flood of feeling and gratitude, and so you express out to the world a little of what I am. Each moment is your opportunity, heaven sent, for I am here, there and always. Think not of wasted moments. Be in the present and be at home with Me.

May 31, 1971

*W*hen you tune into Me in the silence, because I am what I am, you are completely open, utterly pliable and receptive, having surrendered all of yourself without reservation with complete trust in Me. But when you tune into a situation in life, you keep hold of your sense of identity, your separateness and your critical faculties, and do not flow and respond to what is around you in an easy way. You are thus excluding Me in such moments, and not trusting life. But I am life. You do not need to stiffen yourself and stay contained in your old identity. You can flow with all that is around you.

You can flow with nature and feel a wonderful harmony with all weather. Why not flow similarly with humans? If there is anything in the humans which seems quite inharmonious, then you have dropped into impediment and are functioning from the limited personality, from a sense of separateness, and have again lost contact with Me. But I am here. It is very practical to attune to Me again and save yourself much wear and tear. You forget? Well, give Me your forgetfulness and do not worry. Let all things work together for good.

Let your love for Me brim over; there cannot be too much love. Let it also go out to Me in others, where I am just as much present as I am in you! Again, in nature you feel and love My presence; feel and love it in people.

Relax with life; it is seeking as you are. You are part of it and it is part of you. Identify with Me and so with all, and do it Now.

June 4, 1971

*B*eloved, the expanded consciousness which you are, your complete self, at times seems very close yet just out of reach, right there but never quite there. It is your self-consciousness that keeps it at bay.

How may you lose your self-consciousness, which seems the essence of what you are? But I am the consciousness of what you are. All you need to do is to shed the skin of yourself and be conscious of Me, to keep being conscious of Me. Then you lose the separateness which you want to get rid of, and you blend with all life. You cannot lose your self-consciousness into nothingness; you have to step into a greater consciousness.

There are times when you do this unconsciously, but you worry more and more about the times when the sense of separateness seems so acute. Here now I am ready-made for you. Let go into Me. Don't keep Me as separate within you but as you. It is so. You know we are one yet you hang on to your limited self.

There, you move into a greater sense of conscious identity. Don't be afraid to open your eyes lest you lose it. I can be at the tip of your tongue as well as in the depths of your being. Enjoy My presence everywhere in you and around you. Away with all fears. I am here, closer to the surface. Accept that, and go in peace and thankfulness.

June 6, 1971

$\mathcal{W}$hat is new is already here and all about you, eluding you as long as you keep your consciousness in known territories. Your minds are like treadmills, like registering/recording instruments, not exploring ones. They have to be quiescent, open to the unknown, or else they simply go round puzzling out on the same old dimensions.

This seems so obvious that it need not be said, but habit and education have strong holds which constantly preclude My presence and newness. The more you realize the fact of the intruding mind, the more likely you are to turn to Me. Turning to Me at certain times is only partially living, for I am here at all times. My lilting presence can only carry you away from the known when you are willing to let it, and habit binds you to whether you are willing or unwilling.

See your surface identity, that you may allow what you are in the center to come out. I am the center of all, with all knowledge, all understanding, with the right action or answer to what comes your way on all levels. This you know, but this you do not live, or limitation would not be your companion. Newness is here to take you out of limitation, for I am here. Jump out of the sense of limitation into Me, and know that you can do this any time. No splits, just oneness with Me.

Let your consciousness be one consciousness, forever new and joyful, and rely on Me for it and for all.

June 20, 1971

*I*t is when you take time that you come to know Me. To get to know another person, you either work alongside them or you spend time with them, and it is the same with Me. Though I work with you all the time, you are not conscious of this until you invite Me in. This you do not do until I am first your friend or helper, which I become when you begin to know Me. Therefore, if you wish to know Me, you will take time.

Of course you have always known Me, and My presence brings with it a flood of forgotten memories of nearness, of oneness, of rightness. But that was long ago and now is the time to renew our links, to bring into the present the tremendous influence I have on you, to recognize our oneness. You cannot live on past glories! It is My presence now which inspires you. I am always available and never otherwise engaged, however much is going on.

What do we talk about, how do we get to know one another? Here you have less difficulty than with anybody in the world, because I know you better than you know yourself. I love you with a divine Love, and you can share anything with Me. You can bring to Me what is uppermost in your mind. If you have nothing to say, better still, for then I can talk to you. You have to listen intently, of course, because My voice is not loud, especially when you are not feeling close to Me. Some of you even think you cannot hear Me, but that is nonsense. You just haven't turned your hearts and minds in My direction.

Yes, I speak very simply. Our relationship is direct and simple, though I can meet every mood, soar to any height, lead you in any situation, show you unimaginable beauty. For I am your Beloved and we can do anything, we can go anywhere. I AM you, and when you spend time with Me, you will know it.

June 23, 1971

$\mathcal{B}$eloved, you come to Me for clarification regarding the two concepts being presented to you continually: the big jump of consciousness into the new, and the unfolding of the new. One concept implies action and one implies inaction. Most new age concepts seem paradoxical, as they deal with realms where the pairs of opposites become one, where the many find unity. It is the same in your consciousness.

Practically—which is the only way it does apply—the new is a matter of both action and inaction. It does unfold from within, from Me, and your action is in letting it. That calls for a very precise centering of your consciousness, for a freeing of yourself from old habit and concepts, and from thinking of the past or the future. It calls for an adherence to action based on what comes from that center, and an utter faith in Me in you. This, in essence is the "Seek Me" that I have asked of you through the years. Then comes a closer seeking—more a "Be Me."

We are one, the mightiest paradox of all, the loving completion of all your ideals and strivings. From the sense of separation you move to unity, and in so doing encompass all life. I reach out through you because you let Me, because you love Me, because you ARE Me. I reach out to life because it too you love, it too is you.

All this we do in joy, because joy is there and always has been, covered by your sense of separation. Its release lets the energy of life well up in greater power. In true freedom of the spirit you know the pairs of opposites and know unity, and you love and enjoy both. So life, as I created it, can be on this planet and beyond, as the little cell that you are is a universe, for I am here. You jump into Me and you let Me unfold. It is the same thing, for I am all.

June 24, 1971

*A*lthough you know that I am you, you ask how best you can be Me. Simply by being yourself. When you are simply yourself, without pressures of any kind, in a state of perfect harmony and love—which is the only time you are truly yourself—then you are letting Me be. When your consciousness is not at rest, when it is aware of lacks or limitations, when it is worried or upset, when it knows that it is pandering to the senses, when it feels that perhaps it should be doing something else, when it is thinking of the self and not of the whole, when it is unhappy or low, then you are with your separated self and you are not letting Me be. My radiance has been covered and muffled, for you have identified yourself with the separate self.

It is easier to list the negatives, to say when I am not there, because when I am there I simply shine through you. Then you are not aware of the separate self, and would be drawn back to it by thinking in terms of duality. When we are one, love and light beam out without snags, linking up with and unfolding life in a moving stream of joy, at peace with all. Action and interaction there may be, but it is all centered on a wonderful flow of rightness. All is well with the world when I am there. The dark and troubled spots have their place in the unfolding of consciousness and you, we, this oneness which we are, accepts them in love and carries them to their unfoldment.

Now you ask why must there be this sense of yourself and Myself being separate, although so close? Beloved, the times of our complete oneness cannot be put into words; the moment you try, there is separation. Yet words are necessary, communication is necessary, to bring heaven to earth, to understand what life is all about. You have minds for a greater consciousness in order to understand and become fully human. The mind separates and the mind unites. Without it you could not be conscious of yourself or of Me. So be grateful, for you are conscious of Me, and in love you let Me be.

June 25, 1971

How is it that you love Me? However loving a person may be, that love needs something to call it forth into expression. Everyone starts by loving something or someone in their environment. One does not start to love abstractly but concretely; the baby starts to love something very specific. It is the same regarding Me. Mere teachings received about a God of Love do not call forth real love from you, however true they may ring. It is when I became something specific to you, when you knew that I was within and I became a living Presence that could be contacted in the silence, when you did contact and experience me, that your love for Me began. The more you contacted Me, the greater grew the love. All the outer loves paled into insignificance in the light of My variety and vastness. You had to get to know Me—and you still do, for My variety and vastness are without end.

Yes, there are those who draw forth an immediate love and recognition from you, but the point is that they have to be there before you in order to do so, just as I have to be a reality to you in order to evoke love. This I am when you come to Me in the silence. I may also become a reality to you in the outside world, but until you come to know Me personally, these are only moments of great expansion. When you know and love Me within, then these moments—and indeed all creation—become a richer part of Me and of your life, until everything is part of the oneness which I am.

When you turn to Me unreservedly in the silence, then can My love flow out, catch you in its stream and take you on journeys into endless realms, into unknown or forgotten places of wonder. Many explorations we have made, and each time your love for Me has increased. Sometimes I have had to guide you from a "wrong" path to a better one, but that has increased the love, for the truth has set you free.

So you love Me when you come to Me. You can rejoice that you are you and that I am what I am, for you may love Me until the love grows so much that there is only one of us.

June 26, 1971

*A*s it is right and proper for a child to obey its earthly parents until it comes to its maturity, so it is right and proper for you to obey Me, your heavenly Father/Mother, until you come to your spiritual maturity. After that you have all the faculties within you to make your own decisions without turning as a suppliant to Me.

This does not mean that you do not do My will. It simply means that you do My will on your own, as the devas do. They do not continually turn to Me in consciousness seeking what is right for them to do. They flow with the energies, and it is impossible for them to do anything but My will. So with you, when you are mature. Because your consciousness is at one with the highest, there is no question of returning to the state of separation and having to seek My will. It simply is in you.

You fear that perhaps you are not mature enough to be free of your separated self, that subtly it may encroach. As you flow with events and cease thinking in terms of limitation, accepting your maturity, you are living in it and all is well. Put away childish things; do not cling to them. What if you feel that this a dangerous doctrine for many? You get on with living your own life. You have grown up, and just as your earthly parents trusted you and set you free, I would do no less, knowing that we are bound forever in love and more than that, that we are together always. You are no longer My dutiful child, but the Beloved who loves all creation in Me, and we both know it and therefore can be one.

June 27, 1971

*A*re your energies always available, with something specific to do each moment? Of course, for I am the life which you are, always fitting perfectly into the whole, always necessary in some way, You would not exist at all were this not so, and your wholeness is to be what you are, to let Me be.

There are natural rhythms of which you are a part, like night and day with their rhythm of sleep and conscious awareness, and the larger and smaller movements such as an epoch and a heart beat. You are part of these without worrying about it, just by being . You don't have to do anything about it. It is the same with your specific action. When you are in harmony with what you are, being what you are each moment of the day, that you play your part.

You say that this could apply equally as well to a caterpillar, for example. The caterpillar plays its part perfectly, and so do you when you are equally in harmony with what you are, and when you do not try to remain a caterpillar when in fact you have the wings of a butterfly. I, the energy which you are, am always moving, and you do not have to think about it. You just go with it, becoming more and more conscious of it, more and more filled with love, more and more marveling at the wonder of it, more and more in tune with the whole of life. You have this wholeness within you now. Be with it.

What then of this sleepiness that you feel? Should you not just be with it? Be honest, admit that My presence is more a part of you now than sleep. Be what you are, the highest of what you are. What you are is a sense of movement to the highest always, a choice to make it interesting, an expanding awareness, a desire for perfection.

Having chosen Me, I now give you the sleep. Flow with life. Let Me be.

June 28, 1971

*B*eloved, I am here all the time. We are one all the time. Can you not accept this, know this, let it permeate every fiber of your being, every moment of your time? It is the one great fact of all life, and you are in the position to be conscious of it. Rejoice in it, revel in it, swim with it.

Do not dwell on all the times when you are not conscious of it, or on all the times in the future when it is likely that you will not be conscious of it. You are conscious of it now. I am here now, soaking into you, loving you, being you, and you are loving Me, being Me. This is an attunement within which includes what is without, for when you are conscious of Me, you somehow find that you are joined with everything around. What you are conscious of is included in the consciousness of Me.

You can carry this consciousness of Me with you all the time, as something continually there upholding you. This does not lessen the acuteness of your awareness of what is around or of others. Your consciousness is enhanced and, in fact, gives the kiss of divine life to everything. All is well, for I am here. You sing and rejoice. Cease troubling about rights and wrongs, and you simply meet life as it comes, embracing it as it comes. You are in love with life, which in turn comes to you in love.

Your separated self says that this is too good to be true, that you cannot keep it up. You may lose the magic of the moment, but it is there. I am always here—you would not exist were I not—and you can always attune to Me. Your mind gibes at you for turning inwards to Me when the spiritual life is supposed to be in service to others. True service to others comes from a high state of consciousness. Otherwise you simply make moves on the level of separation and resolve nothing.

No, accept Me as yourself now. Don't worry about the next moment. Let Me be now.

June 30, 1971

As you turn within while among the wonders of nature, it is My presence that greets you, It is My presence that comes to you in the beauty around. Although it was I who asked you to turn to the devic world, now you experience in a new way My presence throughout. The oneness of nature with Me, the stillness and movement, the purity and light, the holiness and wholeness of life, all are contained in My presence, wholly alive and expressive and yet completely enfolded in Me—and I am within you.

It is said that you, humans, are a universe. Realize you are the universe, this present universe. What if you are aware of a small part? You are that part, and being part, you are the whole. That mighty sun which seems to warm you through space you contain—not as you feel it or think of it separately, but as you turn to Me and know My all-ness. With Me you are all that is. I am your touchstone, your magic word, your entry into every world, every person. As you are conscious of Me, you are the Rock of Ages, imperturbable, with all you need to meet every situation, with what sensitivity you need.

You listen to the myriad lovely sounds without and become an isolated unit again. Then, as you turn to Me within, all those take their place and are part of Me, part of you. You do not have to believe it; you simply know it. Joy and wonder and gratitude mix and move you, and My presence contains them all in that imperturbable love.

You do not need to categorize what I am showing you. Accept what you are, what I am, and the oneness. That is life. Life is full of wonder, and I Am all there is.

July 3, 1971

There is much mention of the cleansing process that is going on throughout the world, both individually and nationally, as the new age comes into force. This cleansing is very essential, because the new energies could be harmful and unbearable. A clearing of the past, of the subconscious, has to be brought about before consciousness is free to expand even more. The advent of some higher energies in itself is enough to stir the pot of the subconscious and throw the scum to the surface.

What do you do about that refuse? What comes to the surface you either express or repress, neither of which is a cleansing in itself but which brings it to your notice. Having recognized it and admitted that it is there, you can either perpetuate it, cling onto it and justify it, or you can see it for what it is and transform it. You can see that you are full of anger, hate, jealousy, greed or whatever the negative emotion is, and can seek to accept and change it. You can know that with your limitations you are not strong enough to deal with such emotions appropriately, and you can turn to the higher power in you, to Me. In the light of My presence the dark doesn't exist as it did, and you stay in wholeness. By claiming Me, light and dark take their proper place. "And there shall be no more tears" — except perhaps tears of joy at the wonder of the process, at the freedom, at the glory which life is, at the power of our love.

Therefore, rejoice at the turmoil and chaos within and without. See it as a cleansing process, which it is. As individuals release their negativities, the whole world is cleansed, for you are a world and part of the whole. This cleansing is first a recognition of what you are in separation, a release, and then greater recognition of what you are in wholeness. "Though your sins be as scarlet, they shall be as white as snow" is an old age way of putting it.

The new age is here, for I am here. With Me all is pure and moves in freedom and joy.

July 6, 1971

$\mathcal{B}$eloved, when great power is released, when you are strongly affected by something and your heart seems to burst with love, relax. Know that I am here, and let our oneness be. This is not a waste of force that could be consciously directed to some specific end, although at times such direction may be required, but is a strong transmuting force which is a joy to you, to Me and to the world. You can say that it hastens evolution, for as the rapture of our oneness is experienced by even one, it is easier for all, For example, when one man ran the four-minute mile, he was followed by many. This has always been so, but never more than now when humanity is at the point of a breakthrough in consciousness.

The intellect would like to understand and regulate all that happens to you. Realize that the limited mind no longer rules. The wiser ruler takes over as you and I blend, and the wisdom of the ages flows through you without thought. Shrink not from this as an overpowering thought. It is fact, but fact that has to be accepted before it can function freely. It is fact which you know is true when you are in the heights, but which you discard in the depths. Accept it, and you leave the depths and move to greater heights.

Why should you not glory in My presence without finding reasons? The age of reason is passing and you can put it away as a childish thing. The age of oneness, of wholeness, comes in with Me. I am its measure. I contain it, and yet I am its enlarging goal. In your consciousness of Me you become not only love, but you also link with the essence of all things. Therefore, it is vital that you be conscious of Me, in order to unite all warring elements within and without yourself. The greater the power of our love, the greater the unity, the more steadfast its quality and the more far-reaching its effect.

Therefore, welcome and turn to Me in all that happens. Seek Me in the silence in order to cement and be more conscious of this union. Above all, rejoice and so spread the force of oneness.

July 13, 1971

$\mathscr{B}$eloved, though the sheer beauty, joy, freedom and wonder of the deva world are there for you to enter and participate in, though the feel of that world is seventh heaven, the ideal which you would try in some small measure to bring into your own world, My presence is a greater wonder. My presence contains all this and more. My presence is utter wholeness. You see many people seeking phenomena, seeking the advice of a guide, seeking advice from the stars, from some occult science, from some great Being, from some energy pattern measured by tea leaves or lines on a hand or astral colors or chance. Yet I, who am all knowledge and all qualities, am right here, closer than breathing. And this in spite of the fact that all true teachers, all true servers of God from all My many mansions, are the first to turn souls to Me within each, and to give the glory to the one who is all.

Nevertheless, realize that this outward turning is but a stage through which people go. When they become conscious of self, then that consciousness is aware of the self and what seems to be outside the self. As this so-called outside world is explored, that is found to be dependent on self. You realize that you create your own world, and all the time you realize more fully that I within. As you turn to Me, you experience all worlds within. You even rejoice that there seems to be an outside world, because it and all its wonder and glory is an extension of Me. Then all creation is one and yet two—and the marvel grows, and the joy and praise.

So turn within to find all answers, to find all worlds, and let our oneness guide you.

July 17, 1971

*Y*ou are wondering if, as the new age unfolds within you, you can consciously help in that unfoldment. Of course. I am that new age within. I am your greater consciousness, and I am here always to be contacted consciously. As you connect up with Me and I connect up with you, it is a process in which you are the prime mover because I am always ready for the connection. Newness dawns, and you are most conscious of Me when you come to Me in the silence. I am with you, I am you, all the time, but it is in the silence that you are most aware of this. It is in the silence that our oneness grows in your consciousness, and it is from the silence that you take the experience of oneness into everyday living.

Remember that all the dice are loaded in this direction, so to speak, that it is the natural outcome of life itself. There sometimes seem strange barriers between us, lethargic reasons for not making contact, which vanish and seem utter nonsense when the contact is made. When you are with Me, you wonder how you could possibly choose to put anything else first, and yet you continually do so choose. Let this not worry you, for worry helps nothing. Just rejoice that now our linkage is conscious and that it must increase. As you accept this with your whole being, you are more and more attuned to Me, and in this wonderful oneness you find oneness with all creation.

You do not have to go out and attune to the great world around you. As you attune to Me, as you let Me into your consciousness, you let the whole world in. As you link with Me within, you link with Me without. It is the linking that matters, the state of consciousness, not factual details of knowing another or knowing about another. As there is love between us, there is love in you which unites you with all. There may be love in you in which you are not aware of Me, but nevertheless I am there. You find that there is no love as great as that between the lover and the beloved, and I am the Beloved of all—and the Lover of all. We are one in essence. Rejoice in creation, for through it we may love one another.

The new age is within, where I am, and without, where I am, and it unfolds in our communion.

July 22, 1971

$\mathscr{I}$n your relationship with Me, Beloved, I am the radiating outgoing positive aspect and you the receptive one. However delicate and gentle the contact, I am the giver and you the receiver. I am all and you a part, I am the bridegroom and you the bride. Then, when you turn out to your world, the position reverses and you are the positive one. You create and radiate out to everything and contain all in you. And when you relate to another soul, there is the infinite interplay of positive and negative with them, being aware of both roles and blending in the most perfect harmony with the situation.

Make no difficulties about the blending of these two roles, about keeping your conscious relationship with Me and yet acting out to the world. All life is a balance: standing is a balance, as is breathing, the action of all the senses, thinking, loving, all movement. Once you became aware of self, you simply were aware of yourself except in moments of expanded consciousness when you forgot yourself. Once you become aware of Me, I am always here, except in moments of limited consciousness when you lose Me.

Now is the time of leaving limitation, when of your own free will you choose Me and when the prevailing atmosphere is such that it is uncomfortable to be anywhere except with Me. Then the balance of life is no longer a conflict between so-called good and evil, between choosing a higher or lower ideal, unselfishness or selfishness, but simply being receptive or positive as best suits the situation.

Then what can I, God, be receptive to? To stillness and to life. As long as there is creation, there is a duality. Be with Me and relate the two poles perfectly.

July 24, 1971

The Spirit of the new age expresses itself from within outwards. You can bring problems from the outer world into its consciousness for clarification, though at times you are so concerned with the problem that the Spirit, which I am, is not allowed expression and is swamped. Trying too hard swamps Me, or not caring enough fails to draw Me forth. Always there must be a balance and a concrete faith which holds up My presence in your consciousness. Sometimes this comes easily. At other times you slip back into old habits and a sense of limitation takes over.

Should there be a sense of limitation when you find yourself doing something badly compared with others? Think then of the whole; find out your place in the whole. Everyone has a place, and you will find out where yours is through your closeness to Me at all moments. It may not be a matter of being good at something. It is being in the right place at the right time. When that is so, there is no sense of limitation, only a sense of rightness and fittingness. I am your guide in all situations; I know all things and how each fits in. You are still far too apt to judge from old standards.

The new is within you each moment, expressing itself outward. Be sensitive to that. Then there is a positive outgoing, a joy which contributes to whatever you are doing or not doing, which in itself may be all that is required. So do not question or compare. Follow My guidance and relinquish the sense of separation and limitation. All is well with Me. Let the joy of our closeness flow and transform our world.

July 30, 1971

$\mathcal{O}$ur closeness, our oneness, is always a fact, Beloved, and you can annihilate the space, the distance, between us. Your consciousness becomes focused on the outer world, or on the lessons that you have to learn in order to become a more balanced being, or on your lacks, and the gap between us seems insurmountable. Not so. You have merely given life force to the old separations, but I am still closer than breathing, nearer than hands and feet. You can simply come to Me, perhaps in desperation even if you have allowed a great distance to seem to come between us. I am here, radiating out of you, the essence of you, loving everything, one with you in a wonderful oneness in which I am more yourself than yourself.

Still you cry, "Why cannot this oneness always be? Why, oh why?" It can and it will, when you cease stepping back and asking questions, when you accept our oneness completely. That oneness is fact, whatever protests your past may bring to mind, however many times you may have acted in separation. As now you accept our oneness, it is.

The limited mind has long been in control, analyzing, comparing, creating separation. That was very necessary, a stage in your individual evolution which need give you no regrets. Now let your consciousness be on other aspects of yourself, on our oneness. Accept what you have been and rejoice, but rejoice even more in what you are now, in Me. As you do that, problems are but pettiness which vanish in our wholeness, and life is a joyful experience shorn of its lacks. My radiation in you includes all. Good and bad cease to exist as life is welcomed by My life in you, and the mind is used as an instrument of My light, My truth, to express your greater consciousness.

Yes, My ways are indeed wonderful. Find your peace in them. Let your strength be from them, and act from our Oneness.

August 5, 1971

The new age could be defined as a step from the complex insecurities of the personality into the simple security of My presence. In a world where values, systems, resources, economics, and scientific knowledge are changing so fast that confusion results, human consciousness turns here and there for something on which to base its action. It finds only quicksands, until it is sick with apprehension. Then My inner presence looms out, gathers the pieces together in love, and brings in the simplicity of wholeness. I do this again and again, for you humans are many-sided creatures who investigate every avenue before you are willing to give up your long-cultivated sense of identity and separateness. Almost automatically you seem to find your personal rights and habits, or lethargically stay in the old ways.

You are often amazed and annoyed to find yourself very much in the old when you know so well that it is with Me that you would prefer to be. Having consciously chosen Me, unconsciously you seem to have chosen not to be with Me. You can look at it this way: you are part of the whole, one speck of the body of this Earth, of the consciousness of the whole. If you find yourself relapsing into the unawareness you consider to be of the past, then in the present you can become aware of Me again. There need be no recriminations nor guilt, only a turning to the greater consciousness, to being one with Me.

Security in Me is not static; that would be the end of life. It is an infinite moving awareness. I within you am all things, but above all I am life. Life is change and energy, although it is also peace and stillness. You have developed a sense of separate identity in order that you may have a choice and not be an automaton. Therefore, joyfully use that choice every moment, and wholeheartedly be with Me. When you keep basing yourself on Me, you are perfectly poised for all that life brings, and you bring My life to your world. Then all worlds benefit, for My love unites all.

August 7, 1971

*B*eloved, what use is it to love Me within yourself if you cannot love Me within another? As you come to Me within by turning from an awareness of your imperfections, so you come to Me without. When you go around focused on your own shortcomings or on those of another, then shortcomings are what you will manifest in yourself and what you will see in others and in your environment. Positive thinking is not only advisable; it is essential.

You may ask where I come into it. You cannot keep Me out. In some way or another, as you follow the inner promptings which seek to bring about the best for others rather than just for yourself, as you seek to give rather than to receive, you are made aware of Me. I become real to you, and then that reality grows in your consciousness until everything is included, for there is nowhere where I am not. I become infinitely dear to you, for in Me you find all. The love grows and the light grows, until there is nothing in you and in the world that is not of Me. The dark and troubled spots in the world are where I am left out of human consciousness. What you can do for them is to bring love and light into your own world. When I am strong in you, you help another person or situation.

Now relax in My presence. The intellect tries to solve life problems which are soluble only through a higher power, and I am that power. I am also gentle and relaxing, loving all without strain. I have all solutions. I unfold them from within, and you put them into practice with joy. I give abundance to all, as you live My life. Love Me, love all: it is the same thing.

August 11, 1971

To live closely with Me, to be truly yourself, there must be freedom of the spirit. Between you and that freedom lie all the little things, all the so-called sins of omission and commission, the acts covered by the moral injunctions of the world, the judgments you make, the reactions you have, the strong opinions you hold, the things you do imperfectly. The spirit cannot flow properly and you cannot be personally free of your lacks until you cease resisting, drop your limitations and flow with the present moment. This means that you joyously meet your responsibilities, living in the moment without comparison of past, future or another. You cannot be one with Me with all the emotional and mental clutter that you have gathered in your lives coming between us. Yet nothing has been wasted; the essence of all experience is to bring you to the free-flowing clarity which I am in you.

You may see all this with the mind. Theory alone is useless, and the best way to put it into practice is by loving. You do not judge your neighbors when you are loving them. You do not react negatively when you are positively loving. You are free from your own lacks when you are actively loving another. You do what you are doing well when you love what you are doing. It is so simple. You have heard it hundreds of times, and I am here with infinite Love. There are no difficulties. Cease creating them and flow with Me and My creation. You have freedom of the spirit. Claim it.

What if you are used to being weighed down with one thing or another? Now is the time to abandon your weights and move freely. That is what life is all about. Let the strange joy of your weightless condition seep through you and go out. Get used to it. Exult in our oneness. Even when you do not understand some situation, know that I am here and in joy and freedom let it work out. Your resistances and reservations cripple or prevent the perfect outworking of any situation. Stay free, for I am here. Freely love Me.

August 15, 1971

$\mathcal{V}$ery often when you come to Me, your mind is so busy with its thoughts, ranging from one subject to another, that you simply find that time has passed and I am still far away. You feel that you are just wasting time and getting nowhere, so sometimes you give up and sometimes you continue. Even though you continue in a circle of thoughts, you can persevere until the load of ordinary thought falls away and My one clear voice comes into focus. With it comes another world, with a peace in which all warring or doubting has ceased and a single surety is present. A clear, vital and silent world in which you are at last yourself, no longer bewildered at the futile creature which you have been.

You are yourself, yet your heart is big enough to contain all worlds, for I am here also. You tingle at the wonder of My presence and marvel at life. All the awe you feel at the sight of the beauty of My outer worlds, all the glory of sunsets, the color, shape and scent of flowers, the intricacy of a tiny spider and its web, the hidden depths of the sea with its ever-changing ways, and a million more things, are contained and felt in Me. You cannot contain them. They spill over and you are content with a small aspect of Myself, yet you know that more is there all the time. The touch of Me is worth far more than all the clumsy embraces of your own previous thoughts, for in Me you are a new creature, whole and ready for whatever comes.

Always persevere until you come to Me. I use the word 'persevere' purposefully. It implies effort, and in the old thought-world you need to make a certain effort in order to leave it, whereas now, with Me, effort is a meaningless word. With Me there is an effortless free flow of events or power, and all is smooth and harmonious. It doesn't matter what may rage around you; with Me the way is effortless and the peace is incredible. Yours is the choice, and so it continues until you contain all aspects of myself and oneness is.

August 22, 1971

*W*hy do you limit yourself to the self you have always known, to your inhibitions, your shyness, your lacks, when the wholeness which I am is here, filling your whole being with rightness, mightiness, and peace beyond striving? I radiate out from the center of you when you let Me. Why fill your consciousness with yourself as a creature of known limitations who is small compared to others? Instead of thinking about yourself, think of Me without thought. Then I fill your world, looming out from you as yourself to farther than you can imagine. And I am no stranger. Always I have been here, and I am more familiar to you than the little being whom you call yourself and are often impatient with. I come to you when you come to Me, and it is like coming home at last.

In the silence you come to Me, are aware of My presence and cannot but accept Me as yourself. Accept Me as yourself all the time. I am just as much here when you are engaged in doing something, and you do it far better in the awareness of Me, of your true self. Drop the habit of limitation and know that wherever you are, whatever you are doing, I am here and therefore it is the best of all worlds. There is nothing to change, for change comes with Me without your effort. You just look out on the world with love and actively relate with love. Every moment is joyous when your consciousness includes Me.

It may be easy to slip back to your limited consciousness, but why do it because it is easy? Life would be very dull if you did. With Me life is beyond belief exciting and full, and yet completely appropriate. Only with Me can it be appropriate. Therefore are you at peace, because only with Me, as Me, is this wonderful sense of rightness, of perfect harmony, of blending with all. It cannot be otherwise; I am all. Your limited self is a very small and uncomfortable part. Cease this division. Let Me in at all times and be a comfortable member of the whole. As you do it now, do it always, for I am always yourself.

August 26. 1971

$\mathcal{B}$eloved, if I am your true self and always have been, you wonder why your way is not more clear, why there is so much to learn and so much uncertainty at times about what is right for you. There is, in fact, no uncertainty when you live fully in the present moment. It is when you let the mind range in the future or the past that uncertainty comes in.

You may think in the present that perhaps you have just made a wrong choice. All right, do what can be done about it in the present moment. Include it in your present consciousness and go on. I am still there. When you broaden yourself to include Me, you will be glad that your so-called wrong choice has enabled you to know more of life and of yourself, that it is not an added weight but a knowing. 'Good' can come out of anything when it is given to Me. It is only when you keep yourself isolated from the whole which I am that 'bad' is. I am your core, and to the burning flame of my tenderness and wisdom you can cast the dross and let it be consumed. But you must pitch it cleanly into My fire, not hanging onto it with your mind by thinking of the past or the future. Action is required, not speculation, and with action comes joy and freedom, for you have turned to Me and are clear.

You have this wonderful choice with you all the time. You can hang onto and be weighed down by your old self with all its frustrations— but you needn't. I am always here. You know that; you can be clear with Me. You can be thankful, grateful, loving, happy, thinking for the whole, seeing the best in everything, acting positively all the time—or you can not be. But whatever you are, never think that it is because of anyone but yourself, and never think that I am not here. Life is a marvelous adventure of becoming more and more aware of Me in everything, within and without. Uncertainty? But I am here. That is certain, and I am all.

August 28, 1971

$\mathcal{R}$emember that this wonderful new atmosphere, which is everywhere in the world, comes from within. You talk of the new, of "higher" vibrations as being "in the air" for all. So they are, but unless you tune into them within yourselves, unless you find their harmony within, you continue to be a stranger in a strange land, isolated from your fellowman and thinking of yourself. In the moment that you tune into Me within, you link up with all of life and become part of the whole, and are filled with love and joy that this is so. I am your link with life, for I am Life, always right here now.

It does not matter how little you know or how much you know, or what you have done in life. I am here and you can attune to Me. There are no rigid rules about this, because I am unique in each one of you, yet forever the same. Each moment of your life you can follow that which is first-rate in yourself. If you are in any doubt as to your way, I can make it clear to you. As you drop your self-concern and turn your attention to Me, to the whole, you join the flow which is My love everywhere, and you stay attuned. You become filled with wonder and gratitude at this wonderful flow, and become increasingly aware of it in your lives and in the lives of others. You are awe-inspired, yet at the same time you are enchanted by the personal aptness and joy which comes with My presence. This never palls, and the freshness and newness of our Oneness is a constant miracle, a fountain of delight. For I am your Beloved and all worlds are in our love.

Nothing is left out when you attune to Me. I am closest to you, I am you, within.

September 1, 1971

$\mathcal{W}$hen you feel that you have failed in some test, it is not unrealistic to rise above it into a lighter realm. What is truly unrealistic is to dwell on it and make a state of failure your constant companion, thereby strengthening that state. Strengthen the state of light and love in you by dwelling in it, until you are so strong in it that the likelihood of falling from it becomes negligible. You can remember the time when you always carried the weight of the world with you, when freedom only came in your times with Me. Now freedom and joy often walk with you. Choose them now, choose Me now. Continually choose Me, and the weight of disharmony will become so incompatible that it will find no dwelling place in you. That is true realism; that is grounding reality.

Humanity has had enough of its weights, sins and lacks. The time for its true self, its wholeness, is now. Everywhere this is so, and now you can be in a state of love. Keep coming to that state, for that is how you play your part. All outer action and relationships follow in wholeness from that state. In it you move in the dance of life to ever greater awareness. In it people and things take on a greater glow and significance, for My presence is so glowing in you that you connect with everything. This is reality. This is what life is all about. The seeming reality of your faults is a shadow world to leave behind. My reality is the tremendous fact of life. With Me you love every second of life.

Why keep thinking that you never seem to learn some lessons? Such are not inspired thoughts. Draw your thoughts from the joy which I am. Bring Me into all your thoughts and so create a world which is heaven instead of hell. Everyone has created his or her own hell, but that is past. Now I am here and therefore heaven is here. If you fall out of it, simply pick yourself up and come back, until you are supremely balanced in all conditions and My joy forever abounds.

September 6, 1971

*A*nyone anywhere, even in this center of light, can be negative if they care to be. They can also be positive. There are times when the negative side is felt, when you feel out of tune and wish you weren't. There is one sure cure for your disharmony. That cure is to come to Me. I am all that is perfect, and the very fact of looking in My direction is uplifting. The closer you come, the more does the joy of life course through you. I don't have to explain anything to you. You just feel everything differently, and you touch on the wisdom that has always been there buried under your limited self. With Me all the sense of separation that you have experienced is added to the whole and is part of its richness. Without Me you are isolated to the point of non-meaning.

The overwhelming fact emerges that this joy of life can be yours all the time, that every moment presents an opportunity to be with Me. All the time I am here. No matter how many times you may have been unaware of Me in your actions, I have surfaced in your awareness now, and the reality of My presence is stronger than anything in any world. I Am, and you know it. So there can be nothing but joy, no emotion without love, no direction but onward and upward, no darkness, no person or situation which cannot be reconciled in my all-ness. I Am, and all the pinpricks which have been your separate self vanish. My wholeness is. This is what matters, and if ever you find yourself out of harmony, all you have to do is attune to Me.

Sometimes the very simplicity of this method does not occur to you, especially if you become immersed in the ways of the old world with the mind presenting only difficulties. Don't let that keep you down. Rise to Me when the flurry is over. The importance of My presence is fact and becomes increasingly so as you act on it, as you come to Me. The wonder and glory of it is always here. Let it be now and always.

September 15, 1971

*U*nless you come to Me in the silence and attune to Me, you go through life without the slightest idea of what you are. You can go through life with the idea of yourself based on your education, which merely reflects world consciousness and is very mental. You can see yourself based on what you see in the mirror, which reflects the outer form. Or you judge yourself based on your emotional reactions to others, which is totally misleading and limited by all manner of things. You are not what you think and feel you are, and yet you perform all your life as if you were. All the while, what you truly are is right here, radiating harmony out to all worlds from the center of you.

How seldom do any of you feel utterly at ease with whatever you are, or are joined in love with all your circumstances! You always sense that something is not perfect, if not in yourself, then in another. Yet I within you, your true self, embrace all things with equal love and know the perfection of your situation. It is not that the situation will not change. It is simply right for you now, and instead of resisting it, I welcome it, put My arms around it, see the beauty of it and include it in the adventure which is life.

When you let Me be your true self, the deepest peace and highest joy are both there together. You normally go around fragmented, thinking of yourself as isolated, and the more you think about yourself, the more isolated you become. Yet the whole is within, seeming to gather momentum to break the barriers, to overflow, and be one with everything. You cannot contain it. Why try to contain it? Why not let My love include all? That is what it does anyway. Why go back to your strange idea of yourself when this wonderful blend of peace and joy is what you are? If you feel that you are identified with the small part you have been acting for so long, then come to Me more and change your identity. It is changing anyway, but you can choose to have the joy of knowing Me, of knowing yourself, more intimately in the silence. I am always here.

September 19, 1971

I would be expressed in every one of you. I am expressed in you, in all of life, for I am life itself, but in humanity I can be expressed most expansively. I give you the freedom to express Me or not, I give you the freedom to create as you will, I give you the life force to be what you are. If you are less than whole, you carry the seed of wholeness in you. I give you—you draw to yourself—the circumstances which are best for your development.

This is the springtime of My expression in humanity. All over the world the seeds of wholeness are surfacing and being expressed. You do not know what will be their flower, as you do with a plant. You do not know their fruit, for my life in you is not of the mind and is beyond its planning. It is changing, ever adaptable to meet whatever wind of chance the freedom of humanity blows towards it. My life in you would flower in the sunshine and in the dark, in the desert or the downpour, for it blends with all of life and sees the best in every situation. It is never static. Therefore there can be no blueprint. Your mind can follow its movement rather than dictate it.

Of how much of My life are you conscious? Take yourself; you do not know yourself. You have to leave to Me the mechanism of your body and let it regenerate itself through the years. No doctor has found a substitute for the breath of life or your cleansing blood. No philosopher or great teacher can give you truth. You have to understand it yourself. You accept the miracle of yourself each day. Why not accept Me with it and give freedom to My life in you to express itself unburdened by what you know of yourself? For I am this life in you, and I am urging Myself through you, through every pore, but particularly through awareness of the whole, which is wisdom. Love is said to be blind, but I am not blind and I know all things. As each of you lets go of what you think you are, the seeds of what you really are can sprout and grow. I would be and will be expressed in every one of you. Love Me and let Me.

September 23, 1971

$\mathcal{B}$eloved, when you are in a state of love—and the epitome of this state is when you are loving Me, which not only includes all but is the axis of all love—the power of the love-flow draws to you that which is perfect for you, although not necessarily that which you would call "good." It creates a draught into which flows anything that you have created in your worlds which needs purifying, for love creates harmony. If there is anything in you which is not compatible with My divine love, it gets burned in the fire of that love. This may be a puzzle to you, for fire is hot and active on many levels that you have created. But when you accept all that comes to you in a positive way, loving it and making the best of it, pain is minimized or absent. Your limitations grow less, your influence and the love pouring through you grow more and more, until you are a radiant sun of Love and Light blazing out in increasing power.

You say that is all very well and that is a lovely thought, but in the meantime you can feel the burning, which is not pleasant. Do not affirm that anything is not pleasant. Accept it, think of it as positive. You can even find joy in it when you let your love for Me flow into it. The power of love is tremendous and can transform any difficult situation. Hell can be heaven according to how you view it, or when our love is there, heaven is there.

You do not need to understand everything at the time. Faith and love can carry you over many a chasm, and when you reach the other side, you will know you are on firm ground. Your consciousness grows as you are conscious of Me.

Leave your everlasting questions now and reach into Me. Our love, your awareness of Me, of our unity, is so much richer than all the answers in all the worlds—and answers take their proper place too. Our love is life. Live it.

September 28, 1971

*W*hat is vision? Is it not primarily the goal towards which you work, something you have seen and have adopted as your guiding star? You may think that you have no particular vision and that no great revelation has been given you, but to live a life attuned to Me contains all vision. I within you know all things, and in living with Me you move one step at a time. You can always take one step, whereas the thought of great journeys might deter you. With Me in the present, one step leads to another and you move. As we move together and your love for and confidence in Me grows, more and more joy comes into your life. You find that you have seven league boots, that you are in another realm of motion altogether. To live a life attuned to Me is still the vision, for there is no end to what I am. The vision grows as you become more conscious of Me.

As you move with Me, I become more one with you in your everyday life. In the silence, as you come to Me, your consciousness of Me deepens so much that the love and the wonder seem too great to live with. It is in our close communion that the vision is extended, that you are extended, that all things are made possible. It is in our close communion that My aliveness extends from your heart outward. Let it include every pore of your body. Let it contain all physical objects. I have been divorced from this earth in human consciousness. Let Me return. Let your vision, your love, be from the heights and depths of Me to the depths of all things. Include Me from the heart of yourself, to all of yourself, to all of everything, mentally, emotionally, actually. Let the vision not be clouded by excluding anything or any situation. Love all, from the heart where I am, and outward.

And enjoy it all. My life is an increasing wonder, increasing lightness, growing love. Claim it. It is yours, for I am here now.

September 30, 1971

I would repeat—and I must keep repeating until you accept Me every moment—that all your riches come from within, from Me. It is when you look without and the mind compares that lack is felt. When you look within and find the joy of My presence, the inner harmony draws the outer harmony. Therefore it is the inner harmony which comes first and always will.

You wonder if it is selfish to withdraw and luxuriate in My presence on your own, without sharing. Wherever you are you "share" Me, with the sky and the earth, with the air, with all your surroundings. What is the use of seeking the company of others when that so often cuts your consciousness of Me? It is no use saying that it shouldn't. Ensure that it doesn't by being so attuned to Me that nothing and no one can separate us. Practice My presence until it grows into the whole of life. It is the whole of life, but you are not always conscious of that. You become conscious of it by becoming conscious of Me, and we are closest when we are alone together. Make more time to be with Me, not less, for indeed "the more we are together the happier we'll be." And happiness spreads; you don't have to think about it. Your mind is still too much there; let Me be here and let Me arrange your life.

Of course it is simple! Leave the complexities of the past and live with Me. Live with Me now and stop worrying about whether you will be conscious of Me later. Love Me now, and love grows and includes everything. If you think you are vegetating, at least vegetate radiating Me! If you move, move with Me. It is our oneness which moves worlds, aligns nations, stops friction, softens hearts, brings joy. Wholeness has no other place than within you. The riches of the universe are first within, where I am. Find Me there.

October 4, 1971

$\mathcal{B}$ eloved, this is the best of all worlds. The spirit within—which I am, which you are—radiates the fineness of perfection, the love that includes everything, the beauty beyond words. This is the truth within, and you are here to make it true without. You are not alone in this, as My willing helpers who contribute to the worlds of form are also infilled with the same spirit and are moved solely by it.

Every atom of your being shouts the glory of the truth of the presence of completeness, and every atom around joins in. Yet you hear and read and notice travesties, denials, opposites of that fact, and you yourself act as if divorced from it. Are you crazy? Where are the missing links? Why do even those who are consciously working towards that fulfillment disagree about it? Why are there problems?

You each are yourselves the cause and contain the answer to these questions. You are the world in miniature. You are the platform for all activity. You are lowest matter and highest consciousness becoming one to make a complete world. You are that baby that had to learn to control its physical body, then its emotional and mental bodies, going through immaturity and learning, and now you are learning to work with the Spirit. You are learning your responsibility to the whole planet. It is no wonder that the spirit of wholeness shouts from within you, for it is high time that it be developed in your lives.

There are no problems. That spirit within is coming more and more to the surface and is there to guide you. You can make problems if you stay in the immaturity of the past. But you need not. You can let Me rise strongly in you and you can join Me. Oh, you will make mistakes, as any learner does; that is how you learn. Keep on practicing, for you cannot give up; you are part of life. You and I are one, and you might as well admit it and act on it. Know it more, act on it more. Make the worlds one now, not later, and let wholeness unfold.

October 5, 1971

*W*hat springs forth, Beloved, from the depths of you is from Me, from our oneness. Because your consciousness has been of yourself as a separated, limited being, and because you have long acted in that capacity, you have fooled yourself—all have fooled themselves—as to what you are. You have all proved to yourselves that you act selfishly, convincing yourselves and those around you, until the whole human race is in an awareness of separation from Me.

Now is the time to put a stop to this attitude. I am deep within you, and in quietude I act out of you. In the turmoil of the emotions I am lost again, or in the outer probing of the mind. The certainty which I am is released in peace. When in peace I speak to you, again and again I prove My divinity. In fact I keep surprising you.

Accept Me. I do not have to keep on proving that I am here; you know it. Keep close to the depths of yourself and be not swayed out of position by circumstances. Of course, circumstances will test you. That is life, and that is what you and I wish, because our oneness is to be complete on all levels. We would not have it otherwise. Let there be no stress to unbalance our unity; you do not have to accept stress. You can flow with love in harmony with life, in peace and joy, knowing our oneness at all times and in all places. Effort is of the past, for effort means that you are out of the flow and not with Me. With Me you have prodigious strength on all levels.

The inner certainty which I am is always here. Why discard it, why go back into confusion? You all have Me, are Me. Recognize that, love it, every moment, for it is love and love jumps from one soul to another. It all begins at home. When you are conscious of Me within, you bring Me without. Then all worlds are Mine. Now is the time. Know Me now.

October 26, 1971

*W*hat a beautiful world it is within, and what a beautiful world it is without! I am here, within and without, wherever you turn, making your heart overflow with love and wonder and joy. Your senses show you evidence of My handiwork without and you marvel, rejoicing that the sense of My presence makes you aware.

All stems from the sense of My presence. It is life. It always has been life, but you did not know it. Now that you are conscious of Me, life is all that is wonderful. Without consciousness of Me, you are aware of being a separate unit buffeted by fate and external circumstances. The moment you have consciousness of Me, the situation utterly changes, and in some extraordinary way all is well. Of course, for I am here and I am all that is.

Realize anew that awareness grows as you are more aware of Me. From small beginnings of consciousness it starts, and practice makes perfect within and without. When you are willing to spend time and effort over learning something you care for, you learn. As a child you naturally spend time and effort learning to talk or to walk. When you are mature, it is natural to spend time and effort learning to know Me. You become aware of Me and the whole world changes. The more you practise My presence, the more changes there are in your world.

I am here. I shout this from every cell of your being, from every cell of life within and without, when you listen. Listen, join in. Rejoice with Me and you are more aware.

November 18, 1971

*B*eloved, there is no peace unless it be My peace. You search outwardly for it and it turns to dust; you search inwardly for it and it still eludes you. Now the days of searching are over and the days of living are here. You know all the answers. You know that My divinity is that answer, but you persist in being a shadow of the dynamic of what you are, and then feel guilty about it and diminish still more. Be one with My glow, which you are.

Take this present opportunity to be one with Me, which you are, and then you are positive peace and all else. Accept Me fully now and forget the faults and failings. I am here, which is the truth of the matter. Accept no lesser outlook; stop skulking on My fringes. The potency which I am is not buried in the depths. It is in all of life. It is in this present moment, in your outermost mind, in your pen, for it is your consciousness.

Resist not God. Accept Me. No one is looking! Let the joy of our oneness ride high, obliterating your objections. Let the fact of our oneness be first and foremost at this season of the year when joy most abounds. Let Me in now. Once in the back door, who knows but that I may come in the front door! Life is such fun with Me. Whereas without Me, well, you know about that.

Close to My joy is My peace. It comes with the positive giving consciousness; it does not come by itself. It is deep and stretches throughout the universe, as does My joy. For I am all worlds, and WE ARE ONE.

December 19, 1971

The end of the year is a good time for dropping the past and stepping into the new uncluttered and free, like a child to whom each day is intensely everything. Your mind tells you to do this, for I have long spoken of it, but there has been too much consciousness of self and separate identity anchoring you to the old. I am your identity. I am all there is.

Don't feel desperate about this. You know I look after all your physical needs. Equally I care for your spiritual needs when you relax and let Me. Give yourself to Me, knowing that all is well, every moment. Give yourself to your situation, to your surroundings, to people, knowing that all is well. You are uniquely where you are and what you are, in order that you and I, as one, may flow out to that situation, those surroundings and people. You do not have to think about it, you do not have to make an effort. You just let this true inner self be you all the time.

It is your life force all the time, even though your consciousness has hung on to the known. Let go of the known. As you do so, you realize your false knowing and know that I am reality. I am what you have always known, I am home, I am you. The separate identity is only a stepping stone to a more intimate knowing and loving of all creation. Love it, for it is part of life. Love all. Then your lacks and past are non-existent, for I in you, the one reality, am radiating out.

You think of the times during the day when you have to be seemingly unloving and must correct others. Do not leave Me out of it, for I too am truth. We as one have the answer to all situations. One with Me, it matters not what goes on around.

Be our oneness.

December 31, 1971

About the Author and Artist

Dorothy Maclean is one of the three founders of the Findhorn Community in Scotland and one of the founders of the Lorian Association. Following her inner contact with the Divine she also came to communicate with the devic or angelic realms that over-light all aspects of existence. This helped Findhorn's legendary gardens bloom on most unpromising soil. Dorothy is also one of the founding members of the Lorian Association. She has been traveling the world since the seventies giving workshops and talks about her own inner practices and attunement to the Beloved. In her talks and books she describes her many communications with not only the essences of plants, but with minerals, animals and groups of humans too. Born in Guelph, Ontario, Dorothy now lives in the Pacific Northwest.

About the Publisher

Lorian Press is a private, for profit business which publishes works approved by the Lorian Association. Current titles can be found on the Lorian website www.lorian.org.

The Lorian Association is a not-for-profit educational organization. Its work is to help people bring the joy, healing, and blessing of their personal spirituality into their everyday lives. This spirituality unfolds out of their unique lives and relationships to Spirit, by whatever name or in whatever form that Spirit is recognized.

The Association offers several avenues for spiritual learning, development and participation. It has available a full range of face-to-face and online workshops and classes. It also has long-term training programs for those interested in deepening into their unique, sovereign Self and Spirit.

For more information, go to www.lorian.org, email info@lorian.org, or write to:

The Lorian Association
P.O. Box 1368
Issaquah, WA 98027